The whole BIBLE in a year for YOUNG ADULTS

50 LESSONS
FROM GENESIS TO REVELATION!

e625.com

The whole Bible in a year for Young Adults
Howard Andruejol, Eliezer Ronda
Originally published in Spanish
Published by e625® © 2024
Dallas, Texas
United States of America

ISBN: 978-1-954149-56-4

Translated by: David Ortíz
Edited by: Sarah Huge
Designed by: Creatorstudio.net

TABLE OF CONTENTS

"All Scripture is inspired by God and is profitable."

2 Timothy 3:16 (CSB)

We are very happy to bring you this series of lessons from the whole Bible. This series will take you on a fascinating tour of a library that consists of sixty-six volumes, which will allow you to get to know God's character, His perfect work, and His wonderful expectations for us.

Today, many churches have developed the harmful habit of reading the biblical texts in small fragments. If you pay attention, you'll notice that in classes, small groups, preaching, devotionals, and daily reading planners, it has become common practice to read isolated portions of the Bible. This is not necessarily wrong, but if we develop the habit of reading the Bible only in this manner, we run the risk of taking in what we read as snacks and skipping meals, maybe even as if the verses we read are phrases from a horoscope. On the other hand, if we delve into the complete story and take time to notice its details and its application, it helps to ensure that later on we will have a better understanding of those individual texts.

Try this exercise: Ask 10 Christians, of any age, something as simple as, "What is the Bible about?" You will get 10 different answers. Ask them to explain to you how the Old and New Testaments relate and possibly some will begin to hesitate. If you want to go a bit further, ask them to explain to you what the book of Obadiah is about and how it relates to the rest of the Bible and to us today.

These should not be questions that only seminarians or pastors can answer. All believers need to be able to understand them. That is why this material is so important.

The reason for this is very simple. Imagine for a moment a jigsaw puzzle, one that's difficult to put together. Would it have 1,000 pieces? Fifteen hundred? Let's think of a puzzle that has 2,000 pieces and try the following experiment. Imagine now that I take the puzzle box and hide the cover that displays the image we are trying to put together. Then I will ask you to put in your hand randomly and take out only 10 pieces.

Now comes the interesting part: What if we asked you to use those 10 pieces to describe the image? Do you think you'd be able to do it? Of course not! You could make something up, but you certainly would not be able to guess the image as such.

At many churches throughout the continent we asked the same question: What are the most famous biblical texts that all churches know? In every city where we tried this exercise, the response was always the same 10 verses.

Yes, just 20 verses. It appears that our new generations are growing up with only 10 of the 31,130 pieces of the biblical puzzle. And with those 10 verses, we expect them to have a clear picture of God's character, His perfect work, and His expectation toward us. It's impossible. If we base our overall idea on only 10 of the thousands of verses in the Bible, we will undoubtedly develop an image that's false, incomplete, distorted, and disfigured.

Just as it is important to appreciate the fine detail of each piece of the puzzle, it is also indispensable to be able to see the complete picture. And that's what these lessons are about.

We have prepared this book as much as possible as a chronological journey through God's Word, from Genesis to Revelation. It is our hope that once they have an overview of the biblical books, your students will react in two ways.

First, that they'll be able to say, "Now I understand what this book is about!" Each lesson will be effective to the extent that each participant gains a better understanding of the content and purpose of the books of the Bible.

As you will see, since this adventure is designed for a full year of lessons, it is not possible to include all 66 books in 50 weeks. It has been a difficult process to compress, summarize or omit. Moreover, we are convinced that Genesis on its own could take us through 50 weeks! We are confident that we are building a solid foundation, and that we will continue to build on it, with more in-depth studies of the specific books. We are looking forward to what will follow from this.

Second, that by better understanding the full picture, your middle schoolers will now be motivated to learn more about the details. If they can connect each book of the Bible to the complete image of the puzzle, it will make it easier for each individual chapter to make sense. We want to develop devout readers of the Bible, scholars of God's Word. Join them on this tour and help them to explore the richness of each individual biblical passage. Take the time to develop new series about specific books of the Bible, as well as complete biographies of biblical characters.

In addition to considering the maturity and contextual characteristics of each age group, we have chosen a lens with which to look at the books of the Bible in this series. This lens will help us underline the great theological and anthropological themes of the Bible.

Each volume is unique and complementary. Those who travel with us through these four books will certainly have a clear idea of what the Bible is about!

The children's volume was developed around an identity that's outside of this world. The biblical journey will focus on the progressive revelation of God's character. Who is He? How does He present Himself to humans? Knowing God allows us to also know ourselves: What is our natural condition? How is our identity manifested in our behavior? We need to be rescued from our condition, with Jesus Christ being our only hope. To receive Him as Lord and Savior renews us. Who are we now in Christ? How does this transformation manifest itself in our behavior?

The volume for middle schoolers focuses on an unconditional and eternal relationship. The biblical journey will focus on God's initiative to relate to humans. It will highlight the invincible obstacle for man - sin, and Christ's complete victory. The emphasis is on God's faithfulness to man - despite our infidelity - and the closeness that it allows us, only through Christ. What defines God's relationship with us? What should I do to live that relationship today?

The volume for adolescents focuses on crucial decisions. The biblical journey will focus on God's expectations, given our new identity, of lives lived according to His character. We will study the divine perspective in order to make the right decisions in every facet of our lives, the purpose of holiness, and the dire consequences of disobedience. The gospel is not focused on our behavior, but given the Grace of God, our best response is to glorify Him.

The volume for university students is missionary. The biblical journey will focus on God's mission, which seeks to redeem the human being. Special attention will be paid to how God has always fulfilled, and will continue to fulfill until the end, His plan for human beings. Salvation is available to anyone. As part of our new identity, God sends us to explain this gospel to every person, even to the most remote places on the planet. This is our true life's purpose, to live in mission here and now.

On our website, www.e625.com, you will find supplementary material for these lessons. Our goal for the conversations that arise from each lesson is that they be theologically deep and didactically creative.

Of course, all this has been the work of a great team of people involved in the design of the curriculum and instruction. Upon hearing the idea for this series, many friends enthusiastically joined this project. To each of you, THANK YOU for investing in the biblical formation of our new generations!

Let's lead them to know the whole puzzle, to have a biblical image of the person of God, to understand His eternal plan and the response He expects from each one of us.

Let us learn together!

Howard Andruejol and Lucas Leys
General editors

Lesson 1 > WHY IS THE STUDY OF THE WHOLE BIBLE IMPORTANT

Although many believe that the Bible is a single book, the truth is that it is a collection of books written by different authors in different social, geographical, and chronological contexts. Experts in ancient writings have compiled and translated into many languages the 66 books that make up the collection we call the "Bible." It is fascinating to discover how all these books written in such different contexts intertwine their themes to reveal to us the identity of God and His plan and mission for us.

The Bible was written by ordinary authors, but they wrote about extraordinary events. There are several reasons why it is very important that we study the entire Bible.

The first is that the Bible states God's case. It states what God says about Himself. It reveals His identity and His character.

The second reason is that it exposes our most intimate needs and provides wise principles for responding to those needs. Throughout the Bible we have stories of imperfect people relating to God and to each other. These stories show how a perfect God gives imperfect people the opportunity to overcome their failures. The third reason is that beyond our faith, the Bible has affected human history like no other writing. The interpretation of the Bible has divided states, marked maps, and generated wars and alliances. We have the testimony of millions of people through many centuries who have shared over and over how the Bible has affected their lives. The Bible is a book, or library of books, that is impossible to ignore.

Introductory questions to the topic (10 minutes)

After a brief introduction, explaining in your words what you have just read and telling everyone that this will be a full year of studying the Bible from beginning to end, you can share these questions to start a conversation:

1. What are the books fo the Bible for?
2. What books do you think are important to read?
3. Do you have any favorite style of book?

The Bible has different literary styles. It has adventure, horror, poetry, romance, and law. Although the Bible was written thousands of years ago, it is still God's message for us today and its truths still have the power to change our destiny.

Literary Styles (25 minutes)

Find book classics in different categories. Here is a list of ideas:

Adventure: The Chronicles of Narnia or superhero or classic comics like *Twenty Thousand Leagues Under the Sea.*
Poetry: A Latin author like Gabriel García Márquez or Neruda.
Mythology: Hercules, the stories of Percy Jackson, or the Odyssey.
Biography: Such as the biography of a character from the history of your country, or a Christian from history like Luther, Spurgeon, or Madame Curie.
Letters and diaries: *The Diary of Anne Frank.*
Fables: Aesop's classics.
Treatises: University manuals of medicine, law, or any other science.
Chronicles: Books of history.
Essays: Something like "The Writer and His Ghosts" by Ernesto Sábato
Fairy Tales: Cinderella, Tom Thumb, *The Little Prince*, etc.

The idea is to gather as many interesting examples of literary genres as you can. You can also bring children's stories, articles from newspapers, fashion magazines, and comics. You don't need to buy anything—try the public library, or borrow from others.

In your gathering of young adults, pass the materials around the group so everyone can see the examples, then begin a brief discussion.

What types of books do you see here?

Which one caught your attention the most, and why?

Now let's talk about the Bible:

Download from www.e625.com/lessons the illustration sheets with all the books of the Bible to help you identify each section.

The Old Testament has 39 books and the New Testament has 27 books.

The books of the **Old Testament** are divided into five sections and styles:

The Pentateuch (five books): Genesis, Exodus, Leviticus, Numbers, and Deuteronomy (the Law of Moses).

Historical books (12 books): Joshua, Judges, Ruth, 1 and 2 Samuel, 1 and 2 Kings, 1 and 2 Chronicles, Ezra, Nehemiah, and Esther.

Books of poetry or wisdom (five books): Job, Psalms, Proverbs, Ecclesiastes and Songs of Solomon.

Books of the major prophets (so called because they are longer) (five books): Isaiah, Jeremiah, Lamentations, Ezekiel, and Daniel.

Books of the minor prophets (so called because they are shorter) (12 books): Hosea, Joel, Amos, Obadiah, Jonah, Micah, Nahum, Habakkuk, Zephaniah, Haggai, Zechariah, and Malachi.

(It's easy to memorize the numbers in each genre: 5/12/5/5/12).

The books of the **New Testament** are divided into four sections:

The Gospels: Matthew, Mark, Luke and John.

Historical book: Acts of the Apostles.

Epistles:
1- Paul's thirteen letters:
-Written during his travels: Romans 1 and 2, Corinthians, Galatians 1 and 2, Thessalonians.
-Written from prison: Ephesians, Philippians, Colossians, and Philemon.
-Pastoral letters: 1 and 2 Timothy, Titus.
-(Some would also add Hebrews).
2- General Epistles: James 1 and 2, Peter, 1, 2, and 3 John, and Jude.

Prophetic book: Revelation of John.

The Bible provides answers to everyday questions. It describes the fundamental facts of how the universe began and how it will end. It talks about how to make good decisions, how to be at peace when we are in trouble, how to deal with changes, and, especially, how to live a life worth living.

Many think of the Bible as an instruction manual, but it is much more than that. Calling it a "manual" makes it sound like a boring college textbook.

To just learn individual verses from the Bible is like watching a few small scenes of a movie, or just one episode of a long TV series. It might be fun, but we wouldn't really understand where it's coming from and where it's going. We would be left experiencing just a portion of everything that God wants to tell us.

Posters to remember (5 minutes)

Make posters of the following verses and display them in a visible place. Show them and ask different volunteers to read each one of them aloud.

Psalms 119:27

Cause me to understand the way of your precepts, that I may meditate on your wonderful deeds.

Psalms 119:105

Your word is a lamp to my feet and a light to my path.

To discuss:

What does it mean to meditate? (Allow time for the group to respond.)
To meditate is to think about what we read, to discover its meaning, and to apply it to our lives.

The Word of the Lord is what guides us, gives us strength through His promises, teaches us the truth, tells us who God is, encourages us when we feel discouraged, gives us faith, and teaches us to live according to the purpose of the One who created us.

To learn these powerful truths and discern the voice of God we need to read and study God's Word. In doing so we will realize that, although it was written thousands of years ago, we can still identify with it and learn from it today.

Conclusion (15 minutes)

Print the following portion of Psalm 119 and give everyone a copy so they can read it well. Invite everyone to read their copy in silence and to meditate on what they read.

Psalms 119:9-16

How can a young person stay on the path of purity?
By living according to your word.

I seek you with all my heart;
do not let me stray from your commands.
I have hidden your word in my heart
that I might not sin against you.
Praise be to you, Lord;
teach me your decrees.
With my lips I recount
all the laws that come from your mouth.
I rejoice in following your statutes
as one rejoices in great riches.
I meditate on your precepts
and consider your ways.
I delight in your decrees;
I will not neglect your word.

Have at least two volunteers reflect aloud on what they've read.

Close with a prayer asking the Lord that in all the studies that will come He may be the one who reveals His truth. Invite at least two other participants to pray, and instruct them to specifically ask for the Holy Spirit to guide the classes and to fill everyone with hunger for His Word.

Give each participant a copy of Why is the study of the Bible important? downloadable at www.e625.com/lessons.

Lesson 2 > GENESIS

The word Genesis means "start" or "beginning," and the book of Genesis speaks of many beginnings: the beginning of the universe, the beginning of humans, the beginning of sin and suffering, the beginning of a nation separated for God, and the beginning of God's plan to rescue all of humanity. As in the good beginning of any great story, the main characters are introduced and developed:

- God, making everything happen by creating the universe and taking the initiative in calling His people.
- Satan, trying to ruin everything, starting with his appearance in chapter three.
- The first family in the Bible, dysfunctional from the start. Adam, Eve, Cain, and Abel.
- And then, none other than Noah, Abraham and Sarah, Isaac, Jacob and his children, and the death of Joseph in Egypt.

Genesis is an identity story and is believed to have been written by Moses. Its purpose is for us to discover that everything begins with God, and that there is no better way to live than by calibrating our plans with His.

Introductory questions (10 minutes)

After a brief introduction in which you explain in your own words what you have just read, have young adults participate by asking some general questions.

1. What do we already know about the book of Genesis?
2. Does anyone have a favorite story from the book of Genesis? (If no one does, be prepared to tell your favorite.)
3. Excluding God, what do you think the characters in Genesis have in common?

Development (40 minutes)

Genesis has 50 chapters, the same number as this series of lessons. In Genesis we can see two major divisions:

The beginning of all things: 1-11:9.
 Creation: 1:1-2:25.
 Temptation and the fall: 3:1-24.
 Cain and Abel: 4:1-26.
 Seth and his descendants: 5:1-6:8.
 Sin and the flood: 6:9-9:17.

Noah and his descendants: 9:18-10:32.
The tower of Babel: 11:1-9.

The Patriarchs: 12:1-50:26.
Abraham: 12:1-20:18.
Isaac: 21:1-25:18.
Jacob: 25:19-36:43.
Joseph: 37:1-50:26.

(We recommend that you make a sign or poster, or use a blackboard, to write these divisions while you briefly review each story.)

Make it participatory

Divide your group into four subgroups with roughly the same number of participants in each. You will need a blackboard and chalk (or blank paper and markers); two cards: one with the word "mimic" and one with the word "draw"; and a bag with pieces of paper on which you wrote characters or things that you'd discussed in class for the teams to depict and guess.

If your group is very large, you can divide into women/men, or have a small group come to the front, or have a group of participants come to the front and interact with the public, or have a leader for the two teams guide the activity.

Once the groups are formed, have the first participant come up. First they must choose, without looking, one of the cards to determine how it should be depicted (by miming or drawing) and show it to their team. Then, without looking, they will take from the bag what they have to represent (object of creation). If you want to add more, then they must choose a qualifying adjective for said object of creation. It may be that they get "draw," "bear," and "jumping," or "mime," "monkey," and "in love." The possibilities are endless—use your imagination!

Start again

Having everyone remain in the four teams, go back to the summary from the start of the lesson. Print or make cards with the main words that make up the thread of the story (or drawings or images that represent it) to help your young adults pay attention. Ask questions and pause to allow them to reflect so they can get their brains working. If needed, help them out before continuing with the story..
Use these words

BEGINNING - UNIVERSE - HUMANITY - SIN - SUFFERING - PLAN - GOD - SATAN - EGYPT

The most important stories

Now give each team the name of one of the patriarchs and the relevant appropriate biblical quotes. Each team must create a poster or drawing that captures the main things about the character, family, work, and other important elements that make up his story. (Give each group a large white sheet of paper and something to draw with.)

Group 1- Abraham: the promise of the impossible. Genesis. 12:1-5; 15:1-6; 18:1, 9-14; 21:1-7.
Group 2- Isaac: obedience brings blessing. Genesis. 22:1-12; 25:19 -26.
Group 3- Jacob: the power of blessing. Genesis. 26:34; 27:33; 30:22-24.
Group 4- Joseph: integrity and forgiveness. Genesis. 37:3-11, 37:23-28; 39:1-5; 42:6-10; 45:1-9.

Give them 10 minutes to read and put together the story and another five minutes to make their drawing. Everyone must show their work. At the end, have an art exhibition showing what each group has done.

Conclusion (10 minutes)

Some adventures in Genesis seem crazy, but in all of them God shows His character and His desire that we can get to know Him, learning how to recognize Him working in our lives and being at our side. Genesis makes it clear that it is always up to us to trust that God knows what He is doing. He does everything well, although sometimes this is difficult to recognize and understand.

Though we may have doubts, it is always worthwhile to obey Him.

Some of the fundamental ideas of Genesis are:

God reveals Himself in creation: He reveals His love by creating us, and His interest by relating to us as a father.

God is faithful and always keeps His promises: Abraham leaves everything to follow God and discovers that God fulfills His promises.

God shows His grace: Although the patriarchs from Genesis were imperfect, God repeatedly gave them opportunities to relate to Him. When they obeyed God they lived great adventures and saw His promises come true. When they disobeyed, they went through great hardship and experienced much suffering.

God is merciful: Joseph remained faithful to God and always strived to do his best, even in the worst situations. God had mercy on Joseph and blessed him in everything he did. Joseph recognized God's mercy and was able to, in turn, be merciful to his brothers.

Give each participant a copy of Readings of Genesis downloadable at www.e625.com/lessons.

Lesson 3 > EXODUS

Exodus means "departure" or "exit." The title refers to the escape of the Hebrews from Egypt on their way to the promised land. This book tells the story of the Israelites beginning right where Genesis ends. The people of Israel that had been received by Pharaoh in Joseph's time had multiplied so much that Egypt had turned them into a nation of slaves.

God prepared a rescue plan that started with a baby: Moses. The liberation of Israel from the hands of the Egyptians was only the beginning of a much greater plan, a plan of redemption, adoption, and the building up of a nation chosen as God's people. The book of Exodus is fundamental to understanding the ensuing books that make up the "pentateuch," or the first five books of the Bible (written by Moses) and also known as "the law." These books tell the beginning of the history of the people of Israel, the establishment of its constitution, and its first administrative, hygienic, and coexistence laws. All of this impacts what kings, prophets, and even Jesus Himself experience in the rest of the Bible.

Introductory questions (10 minutes)

After a brief introduction in which you explain in your own words what you have just read, have students participate by asking some general questions.

1. If you had to go right now to another city or another country with your entire family, where would you go and why?
2. If you had the chance to build your ideal house, what would it be like (bedrooms, game room, swimming pool, etc.)?
3. If you were the owner of the house and had a very large family, what rules would you set?

Development (25 minutes)

We can categorize the 40 chapters of the book of Exodus as follows:

Israel and the liberator: 1:1-18:27.
Slavery in Egypt: 1:1-20.
Liberator in training: 2:1-4:31.
Moses and Pharaoh (the 10 plagues): 5:1-11:10.
Passover and Exodus: 12:1-18:27.
The sanctuary, the priests, and the Ten Commandments: 19:1-40:38.

Below you have a story to quickly tell the tale of the exodus using some young people to act as the story is told. Choose participants you know will not be too shy to act a little bit. If you want, you can prepare signs with each role to be played, and have them ready with a piece of tape. As you designate roles, stick the signs to each participant's chest.

Variation: If you don't have enough participants, replace actors with drawings or cutouts. Cut out pictures of people from magazines and present them as Egyptians and Jews of that time. Keep in mind that you will need to move through the storytelling quickly to help everyone stay engaged. The actors will need to pay attention to the story and act spontaneously as they listen to you.

Characters:

Pharaoh: a leader
Baby Moses: a baby doll and crib
Moses' mother
Moses' sister
Pharaoh's daughter
Guard
Adult Moses
Aaron
Zipporah
The people of Israel: the rest of the students

As you read the story, the characters have to spontaneously act out what you say. Pause occasionally so they can repeat the phrase or react to what they have to do. Let them be creative! Remember to move through this energetically and quickly.

Story of an escape

After Joseph died in the book of Genesis, the Jews who stayed to live in Egypt multiplied greatly (those who play the people of Israel can make a prolonged, "ooh," or say something funny). A new king named Pharaoh, who had not met Joseph, arrived in Egypt (Pharaoh stands up), and he was afraid that he would not be able to control the Jews. Pharaoh forced the Hebrews to do all kinds of slave labor (Pharaoh punishes the Hebrews), forcing them into construction and other difficult jobs. In addition, he ordered: "Throw all the male babies of the Jews into the river." It was then that Moses was born. His mother hid him for three months. When she could no longer hide him she wove him a basket and put him in the river. When Pharaoh's daughter went down to bathe in the river, she found Moses in the basket and saved him from being killed. She adopted him and took him with her to her palace.

One day, when Moses was of age, he went to see his blood brothers. He saw a guard whipping them (guard mistreats the crowd). Moses hit the guard, killing him. Moses hid the guard's body in the sand (Moses kills the guard and hides the body). The news of what he had done spread quickly. When Pharaoh found out, he planned to kill Moses, so Moses fled Egypt. Arriving in Midian, Moses once again became a defender of the poor, helping some women who were being harassed by a group of shepherds. The women told their father what Moses had done, and he received Moses into his house. Moses then married one of these women: Zipporah.

One day, when Moses was taking his father-in-law's sheep to pasture, he saw that a bush was on fire but was not burning up. As he approached, the bush called to him: "Moses! Moses!" Moses came closer. Then the burning bush, which was God, said to him: "Take off your sandals, because you are walking on holy ground. I am the God of your Father, I am the God of Abraham, Isaac, and Jacob. I saw my people suffering, I know their sorrows" (people act out suffering). "So I will deliver them from the Egyptians, and bring them into a good and spacious land. I will send you to tell Pharaoh to bring the Israelites out of Egypt." To which Moses replied: "Why meeeee?" God said, "Fear not, I will be with you." God also sent Aaron to meet Moses and help him confront Pharaoh. Finally, Moses and Aaron came before Pharaoh and said to him, "This is what the Lord, the God of Israel, says: 'Let my people go so that they may celebrate a feast in my honor in the desert.'" And Pharaoh answered, "Who is the Lord? And why would you distract the people from their work?" He drove them out of his presence and then gave more work to the Jews, who got angry with Moses (crowd boos).

Moses complained to God and doubted Him, but God responded, "Now you are going to see what I am going to do with Pharaoh. Only through my powerful hand will he let the people leave, only through my powerful hand will he drive them out of his country. And when I display my power against Egypt and bring out the Israelites from there, they will know that I AM the Lord."

Thus the plagues came to the people of Egypt, including pestilence, insects, and diseases the Egyptians had to suffer for not freeing the people of God. Then came the hardest plague of all, which was the death of the firstborn of every family who had not marked the doors of their house with the blood of a lamb. After this, Pharaoh, who had lost his own firstborn, finally let Israel go (young adults stamp their feet on the ground pretending to march).

A pillar of cloud guided them during the day and a pillar of fire at night showed them the way to the promised land. When the Israelites had been on their way for several days, Pharaoh regretted letting them go: "What did I do? Who is going to do the forced labor now?" He took out his horses and went after the Jews. The Israelites, who were then facing the Red Sea, felt betrayed and trapped, but God had a plan. The columns that were in front of them moved to the back, between the Jews and the Egyptians, and Moses extended his arm over the sea. A strong wind divided the waters in two. When all the Israelites had finished crossing the sea, Moses extended his arms again, and the waters closed, destroying the Egyptians who came after them.

Thus, the Israelites embarked on their true path. God freed them from their past slavery and they walked with Him toward His promises.

Let everyone give themselves a round of applause.

The Ten Commandments (15 minutes)

In the midst of this adventure, God gave the Hebrews 10 laws that became a historical frame of reference for all humanity.

Ask a volunteer who can read well to read aloud carefully and slowly from Exodus 20:1-17, inviting everyone to meditate on what they hear. Then resume the conversation.

Ask these questions:

- • What motivated God to give the people commandments?
- • Which commandment would have been the most difficult to obey during that time?
- • Which one is the most difficult to obey today?

Conclusions (10 minutes)

This is the story of God and Moses, and the next chapter in the story of a nation that was called to have faith.

The book of Exodus describes the life of a leader who, even though he often had doubts and asked God not to make him the one to free Israel from Egypt, was obedient and was able to be part of God's great plan for His people (7:6). God formed a friendship with Moses (19:20; 24:1-2, 12; 33:11).

In Genesis, God promised Abraham that the number of his de
scendants would be as large as the stars in the sky, and as the grains of sand on the seashore. In Exodus what began with one man ended with millions of Jews leaving to occupy their own territory. **God fulfills His promises (6:8)**

Exodus presents a God of mercy who saw the suffering and listened to the prayers of His people. It tells the story of a God who chooses leaders who, even if they are afraid and make mistakes, must learn to trust Him. The plagues displayed God's power, leaving no doubt that God had authority over creation. The Ten Commandments were clauses of protection for the people to follow to have good interactions with each other and, above all, to take care of their own hearts.

Perhaps the best summary is found in this text:

"Then the Lord came down in the cloud and stood there with Moses and proclaimed his name, the Lord. And he passed in front of Moses, proclaiming, *'The Lord, the Lord, the compassionate and gracious God, slow to anger, abounding in love and faithfulness, maintaining love to thousands, and forgiving wickedness, rebellion and sin'*" (34:5-7).

Give each participant a copy of The Ten Commandments, downloadable at www.e625.com/lessons.

Lesson 4 > LEVITICUS

The Levites were the tribe of Levi, who was one of the 12 sons of Jacob. The book of Leviticus gets its name because it refers to everything related to the Levites.

This tribe was entrusted with priestly tasks and this book receives this name because it gives particular emphasis to the priestly functions required for man to approach God in a holy and reverent manner.

The book of Exodus culminated in the construction of the sanctuary and the book of Leviticus is the instruction guide for how the Israelites should use that temple. Throughout this period, the people of Israel remained in the same place, learning to obey and please God. Leviticus established a code of holiness for entering the presence of God and worshiping Him. Leviticus also presented a God who wanted the people to develop an identity that differed from that of their neighbors.

The instructions in Leviticus were revealed by God to Moses (who was also from the tribe of Levi) and they show how meticulous God is and how imperfect men are. By learning these laws, the people not only had an instructional guide but a reminder that they continually needed to depend on God's mercy. Through the law we can understand in a greater dimension the wonderful work of Jesus Christ on the cross as a perfect and eternal sacrifice, through which today we have direct access to the presence of the Holy One.

Introductory questions (10 minutes)

After a brief introduction in which you explain in your own words what you have just read, have young adults participate by asking some general questions.

> 1- How did you get into your college or choose what you decided to do after high school, and how was your experience in changing your environment and friends?
> 2- What characteristics do good friends have?
> 3- What are laws good for?

Development (25 minutes)

The book of Leviticus can be categorized as follows. (You can show these categories on a poster or write them on a whiteboard.)

1- How to approach God: 1:1-18:30.

The laws of sacrifice: 1:1-10:20.
The laws of purification: 11:1-15:33.
The laws of atonement for sins: 16:1-18:30.

2- How to have a relationship with God: 19:1-27:34.
Holiness: 19:1-25:17.
Obedience: 25:18- 26:46.
Offerings to the Lord: 27:1-34.

Aaron, Moses' brother, was the first priest of Israel. He and his sons were from the tribe of Levi and the book mainly refers to their role.

Divide the group into smaller groups.

Let them join with their best friends in groups of four or five students, preferably with those of the same gender.

Choose one person from each group to lead the questions. Groups can only discuss for five minutes per question, so they must start quickly and speak briefly. When the five minutes are up, notify the groups to move to the next question.

The guide can decide who will answer in what order, if everyone wants to share. They should allow time for as many people as possible to answer each question.

Another member should take notes. These don't have to be detailed, but should include enough to remember what was said and share with the larger group later.

Give each group the Leviticus questionnaire, which you can download at: www.e625.com/lessons.

Review their answers out loud with them, managing the time appropriately.

Conclusion (15 minutes)

In Leviticus, God gave the Hebrews a detailed list of expectations about conduct in order for them to live with Him and with each other. He did this for two reasons. The first was so they could understand how special God is and how they should honor Him. No one can be a good friend unless he first respects himself, and in the case of God, no one can be treated in higher esteem than the Lord. Second, He did this so His people would learn to get closer to Him, to get to know Him. He wanted to be close with them.

Through His commandments, God helped the Israelites to live better, to be better people, and to be holy as He is holy. Meanwhile, the Lord was also preparing the way for them so that in the future everyone would clearly become aware of their need for a savior. Jesus was the only one who could obey all the rules and thus give us free entry into the presence of God, without any more need for sacrifices.

Leviticus is the first great legal exposition. It helps us understand how much we lacked before we had a perfect Savior and Messiah. Jesus was that perfect sacrifice, the one who erased all man's evil by forgiving us and reconciling us with God, settling every affront against the rules of the Levites.

Close with a three-part prayer that you can assign to three different students.

Have the first student recognize who God is and how He deserves all the glory.

Have the second student thank God for His rules.

And have the third student thank God for saving us when we don't measure up to the rules.

Download the daily readings "In the Family" from www.e625.com.

Give each participant a copy of Readings from Leviticus at www.e625.com/lessons.

Lesson 5 > JOSHUA

Joshua is the first of the "historical books" after the Pentateuch. The story picks up right where Deuteronomy ends. After the death of Moses, the leadership of Israel passed into the hands of Joshua. God and Moses were confident in trusting Joshua because Joshua had shown early on that he trusted God and respected authority.

In the book of Numbers we learn that Joshua was one of the 12 warriors who went to spy out the promised land. Although they encountered walled cities and large armies, he and his friend Caleb were the only two who did not cower. That is why God's first order to Joshua was to finally take the promised land. Up to this point, the Israelites had been a nomadic people, roaming for 40 years in the desert. But now what had been promised would be fulfilled. The book of Joshua recounts all the battles that Joshua and the Israelites fought to conquer the promised land, and it ends with the death of Joshua at the age of 110.

Joshua was a great leader who knew how to love God, fulfill His commandments, and guide a great people to their destiny.

Introductory questions (10 minutes)

After a brief introduction in which you explain in your own words what you have just read, have the students participate by asking some general questions.

1. If you could choose today what type of work to do, what would you choose?
2. Who do you know who works in this field, and who perhaps is your role model?
3. What do you know about the story of Joshua?

We all aspire to do or to become something special someday. Over time our ideas of what this means change as we discover new abilities and talents and our interests shift.

Development (20 minutes)

The book of Joshua can be structured as follows:
1. The promised land: 1:1-5:15.
2. Conquest of the promised land: 6:1-12:24.
3. Distribution of lands: 13:1-22:34.
4. Joshua's farewell: 23:1-24:33.

Most of us are attracted to the idea of being the hero in some situation or having some extraordinary ability, but almost no one enjoys the hard labor required to learn the skills that are necessary to respond as heroes in those circumstances.

In Joshua, we see the fulfillment of God's promise to free the Israelites from the hands of their enemies and to lead them into their own prosperous and abundant land where they could become a stable nation. Before this could happen, much preparation and effort had to occur behind the scenes for Joshua to become the leader that God's people needed.

In the previous books of Numbers and Deuteronomy, we can see how the Lord began to train Joshua to fulfill his purpose.

Active reading: Prepare in advance some large signs, writing the highlighted words in the text. You can put them on a wall or a blackboard.

1 - Have someone read Exodus 17:9-12
Joshua was Moses' **assistant**, and while it was a privilege, living in the shadow of a great leader can be difficult and not much fun. Many times he accompanied Moses to his meetings with God, but he always had to stay behind, holding the coat outside of the party, waiting for Moses. Moses asked Joshua to choose some men and go out to fight against the Amalekites who were coming to attack them. As long as Moses raised his hands, the Israelites were winning, but when he got tired and put his hands down, the Amalekites would start to win. In verse 14 the Lord makes sure that Joshua hears how they won the battle. The Lord was showing Joshua his faithfulness and his actions, while increasing Joshua's faith. Joshua showed courage and submission to his authority, which was Moses..

2 - Have someone read Numbers 13:2-3
The Lord ordered Moses to send several men to explore the land the Lord had promised them. After 40 days they returned to report what they saw. They described a very good land with many fruits, but one that was full of giants and surrounded by many towns of residents with whom they would have to fight. At this, everyone became discouraged and began to complain, "Why did we leave Egypt?" Along with Moses and Aaron were two of the **explorers**, Caleb and Joshua. They tried to encourage the people by telling them that with the Lord on their side they could conquer the land. But because of the people's complaining, none of those over 20 years old were ever able to see the promised land other than Caleb and Joshua, who were allowed to because of their courage and their trust in the Lord. In Numbers 14:6-8 and 30 Joshua showed that he learned the lesson of faith. **He trusted God.** He also showed confidence by taking risks for everyone along with his companions.

3 - Have someone read Numbers 27:18-23

The Lord already started granting Joshua **authority.** He had him anointed so that when Joshua gave orders to go to war, everyone would follow him, and when he had them return, everyone would obey. Joshua was still under the leadership of Moses, but the Lord had already begun to give him authority due to his faith and obedience. Joshua showed **humility** by remaining under Moses' command even though he had been given a lot of authority.

4 - Have someone read Deuteronomy 31:23

The Lord affirmed Joshua by telling him to be brave and that he would lead the people to the promised land. God promised to be with Joshua. Joshua received a purpose that later would be fulfilled in the future; **he knew how to wait.** While he continued to fulfill his role. God was preparing him.

5 - Have someone read Deuteronomy 34:9

God filled Joshua with **wisdom,** and the Israelites obeyed him. Under his leadership they did everything the Lord had commanded them. God gave him the final touch he needed to become a good leader: wisdom. Judging by the results, Joshua remained faithful to the Lord in all situations. Joshua was a wise leader.

The most outstanding stories (15 minutes)

Divide the group into six, and give each smaller group one of the following passages to read. They are very short readings, ranging from six to 15 verses.

The Adventures of Joshua:
     Group 1- Joshua 3:5-17: the crossing of the Jordan River.
     Group 2- Joshua 6:3-17 and 6:20-21: the conquest of Jericho.
     Group 3- Joshua 8:3-8; 8:18-20 and 8:26: obedience and victory.
     Group 4- Joshua 10:9-15: the hail, the sun, and the moon.
     Group 5- Joshua 11:16-23: promises fulfilled.
     Group 6- Joshua 13:1; 6-7 and 23:1-8: Joshua's end.

Quickly ask each group to share the story that they read. If your group talks a lot, ask them to be very brief, or set a timer and challenge them to tell the entire story in 90 seconds. Let them prepare for it. Always think strategically when handing out readings.

Conclusions (10 minutes)

Joshua was faithful, brave, humble, and wise, and the Lord rewarded him with much more than he could have ever imagined. Under Joshua's leadership, God's people finally became an organized nation with their own territory.

Let the group share what these four virtues mean to them.

College-aged people are going through a stage in which it's very important to define their vocation and have a vision of their future, and these four characteristics are essential for them to be able to fulfill their mission on earth.

Close with a time of prayer thanking the Lord for the teachings of the book of Joshua, and asking that the entire group can learn to develop these virtues.

Give each participant a copy of Readings from Joshua at www.e625.com/lessons.

Lesson 6 > JUDGES AND RUTH

Joshua conquered almost the entire territory of the promised land. He organized the people of Israel by tribe, with each tribe in a designated territory. For a while the Israelites continued taking possession of the land, but when Joshua's entire generation died, the new generations began to forget what God had done for Israel.

God's people began to adopt the customs and the gods of the people they had conquered, and then they began to live with the consequences of these bad decisions. In the midst of this situation, "judges" emerged, leaders who tried to retain the people's moral values along with God's blessing. This was a period of internal struggles and rebellion.

Right in the middle of this time period, we encounter the story of Ruth. Infighting and mixing with pagan values had weakened Israel politically and spiritually, and in Judges 17:6 we read, "…everyone did what they wanted." The story of Ruth is refreshing because it is full of love and loyalty. Ruth's story shows that being part of God's people is not a question of ethnicity or race but of faith.

Ruth was a Moabite, married to an Israelite. When she became a widow, instead of returning to her home in search of a new husband, she decided to follow her mother-in-law, Naomi, to Bethlehem. There she had her love story, marrying Boaz. They had a son named Obed, a grandson named Jesse, and a great-grandson named David, who went on to become none other than King David. Ruth's story begins with an uncertain present and ends with a bright future, with King David and the dynasty of Jesus Himself.

Introductory questions (10 minutes)

After a brief introduction in which you explain in your own words what you have just read, have students participate by asking some general questions.

1. When someone we love hurts us, how does it make us feel?
2. Is God obligated to forgive us every time we sin? Why do we believe God has no difficulty forgiving us?

God always loved His people, but His people did not always love God. During this period in history we see how the people turned their backs on God. God forgave them and gave them new opportunities and also warnings about what would happen when they became contaminated.

Development (25 minutes)

The book of Judges is structured as follows:
From conquest to defeat: 1:1-3:6.
History of the judges: 3:7-16:31.
A nation without a king: 17:1-21:25..

And the book of Ruth can be structured like this:
Elimelech and his family leave for Moab: 1:1-5.
Return to Bethlehem: 1:6-22.
Ruth and Boaz: 2:1-4:12.
Genealogy of David: 4:13-22.

It is always good to show these outlines on a poster or write them on a whiteboard, illustrating for participants a complete overview of the content you are analyzing.

The four fundamental readings:

1. Have someone read Judges 2:7 and 2:10-14 aloud.
The book of Judges begins just after Joshua has died. God's people turned away from Him again and again. This caused them to make very bad decisions and the consequences fell on them without mercy.

2. Have someone read Judges 2:1-3.
Whenever the Israelites found themselves in trouble due to assimilating the values and customs of the people around them, they would come back in repentance to beg the Lord to deliver them. Their false gods could never do anything for them as they were not real. The same thing is repeated Judges 6:7-10. It seems that the Israelites had very poor memories!

3. Have someone read Judges 2:16-19.
Repeatedly through the eras of different judges and prophets, God rescued His people from living the wrong way. As a result, the people would return to God. But as soon as the person who rescued them died, they would again go after other gods and return to misfortune.

4. Have someone read Ruth 1:6-17.
(Before reading it, explain that Naomi's children had died and that's why this conversation between Naomi and her daughters-in-law happened.)

Being part of God's people and inheriting His promises has nothing to do with our place of birth, but it has to do with our decisions.

Questions to reflect on over the four readings:
1. Why did Israel forget God?
2. As seen with the example of Ruth, the problem was not one of mixing with other people, but of conforming to their values and their vision of reality. Which pagan gods of culture do we allow ourselves to be seduced by today?
3 Why did the people depend so much on their leaders?
4. What is the great lesson hidden in Ruth's example?

Two important interviews (15 minutes)

Separate the group between men and women.

Give the men the story of Gideon (Judges 6:1-10, 36-40; 7:1-22), and give the women the story of when Ruth meets Boaz (Ruth 1:18-2:23).

Each group must read and then choose one person to represent the main character of their reading. The group must then prepare questions for the main character as if they are going to have a TV interview with them.

Control the time so that the preparation does not take long. Students must ask at least four intelligent questions about what the character experienced and, more importantly, how the character felt and what the character learned. The selected person will sit in a chair at the center of the group and answer the questions, as if they are Gideon and Ruth.

Conclusions (10 minutes)

God shows us through these stories in Judges and in Ruth that He loves His people so much. He does not want their hearts to be contaminated with values and habits that will end up causing them a lot of pain and cause them to lose their faith.

God gave His people many opportunities, but He also warned them of the consequences of forgetting Him, which is why He sent leaders to correct them. The stories of Gideon and Ruth, and also that of Samson and other judges, teach that we cannot abandon God when things get difficult, and that remaining faithful during difficult times always has its reward.

Ruth's story makes it evident that God cares more about where we go than about where we come from, and that following Him is a personal decision. Close the class by thanking God for the teachings of the books of Judges and Ruth.

Give each participant a copy of Readings from Judges and Ruth at www.e625.com/lessons.

Lesson 7 > 1 AND 2 SAMUEL

Samuel is a prophet who appeared just after the period of the judges, and made the transition between that time in Israel's history and the period of the kings. A prophet is someone who speaks to the people on behalf of God. Since that time, prophets have personified the spiritual guidance of Israel as instruments of God to communicate His will.

Samuel was a miracle for Hannah, his mother. Until she conceived Samuel, Hannah had been considered sterile. For that reason she dedicated him to God in gratitude. Eli was a priest at that time and at Hannah's request he educated Samuel in the temple. Then God called Samuel as a child, and in his youth and adulthood used Samuel as a spiritual leader of Israel. After many years, influenced by the other nations of the earth, Israel asked Samuel for an earthly king.

Samuel anointed the first king of Israel, Saul. Samuel was the last of Israel's judges. The first book of Samuel ends with the death of Saul. The second book of Samuel tells of David's coronation and the great stories of David as king.

Introductory questions (10 minutes)

After a brief introduction in which you explain in your own words what you have just read, have the students participate by asking some general questions.

    1- If you could choose to be in a position in government, which one would you want?

    2- What would a country be like without a president?

    3- Why do you think we need to change presidents from time to time?

The Israelites had never had a king. They had had great leaders like Moses who had led them out of Egypt, Joshua who had organized them, and the judges who had guided them regarding the laws and commandments of the Lord. The last of these judges was Samuel, and he was the priest and prophet of God who gave Israel its first king: Saul. This is the beginning of another stage in the life of the Hebrews, when new adventures and stories were being written.

Development (30 minutes)

We can categorize the two books of Samuel in the following way:

The arrival and calling of Samuel: 1 Samuel 1:1-7:17.
Saul, the first king of Israel: 1 Samuel 8:1-15:35.

A new king according to God: 1 Samuel 16:1-31:13.
The life of David: 2 Samuel 1:1-21:14.
The last days of David: 2 Samuel 21:15-24:25.

Now let's get to some of the main readings:
Acting with readings from Samuel
Explain to participants that you are going to read some key parts of 1 and 2 Samuel and you need volunteers to role play the characters. If the reading says, "God called him: Samuel, Samuel," whoever does the voice of God must repeat it. For a longer reading they can paraphrase the passage in their own words to make it funny and memorable. In this exercise, the acting must be fast and your story must also be exaggerated to make it fun.

1- 1 Samuel 3:1-10 and 19-20
Characters you need: Samuel, Eli, the voice of God.
Question to discuss: How can we discern God's voice?

2- 1 Samuel 8:1-8
Characters you need: Samuel, the elders of the church (all), the voice of God.
Question to discuss: Why did the people want a king?

3- 1 Samuel 10:20-27
Characters you need: Samuel, tribes (all), the voice of God, Saul (the tallest).
Question to discuss: Why didn't Saul feel self-confident?

4- 1 Samuel 15:10-23
Personajes que necesitas: Samuel, la voz de Dios, Saúl
Characters you need: Samuel, the voice of God, Saul.
Question to discuss: What was the main reason God became angry with Saul?

5- 1 Samuel 16:1, 5-14, 18-19, 21-23
Characters you need: Samuel, the voice of God, Jesse and his sons (only the three he mentions), and David.

Question to discuss: What was God's purpose in having David serve Saul for a time?

6- 2 Samuel 11:1-5
Characters you need: David, Joab, the voice of many, and Bathsheba (this performance can be somewhat embarrassing and very funny).

Question to discuss: What are David's mistakes in this scene?

Conclusions (10 minutes)

In the books of Samuel we find the best-known stories of the first two kings of Israel: Saul and David. The first king, Saul, had the right external characteristics but an insecure heart. The second one, David, began without even having the size and experience to be a king, and yet he had the right heart.

The other two main characters in these books are Samuel himself and Jonathan, Saul's son, who ends up becoming David's best friend. Samuel was the last of Israel's judges, and the one who anointed the first kings of Israel and worked to be their spiritual conscience. The first king, Saul, lost God's favor by disobeying. Then David took Saul's place, starting out as a little boy in the service of the king but later becoming one of the most powerful kings, one with a heart according to God.

In 2 Samuel all the stories of King David are told, the good ones and the others, because David also made many mistakes. But unlike Saul, David was genuinely repentant. He not only served God and had a position leading the people, but also trusted God and loved God's people. For these reasons God blessed David with the following promise, making an eternal covenant with him:

2 Samuel 7:12-16

"When your days are over and you rest with your ancestors, I will raise up your offspring to succeed you, your own flesh and blood, and I will establish his kingdom. He is the one who will build a house for my Name, and I will establish the throne of his kingdom forever. I will be his father, and he will be my son. When he does wrong, I will punish him with a rod wielded by men, with floggings inflicted by human hands. But my love will never be taken away from him, as I took it away from Saul, whom I removed from before you. Your house and your kingdom will endure forever before me; your throne will be established forever."

And so it was, because from the descendants of David, Jesus was born, and his kingdom lasted forever.

Close the lesson by thanking God for including stories of success and failure in the Bible so that we can learn from both. Ask Him for discernment so that we, like Samuel, can learn to recognize God's voice..

Give each participant a copy of Readings from Samuel at www.e625.com/lessons.

Lesson 8 > 1 AND 2 KINGS

The books of 1 and 2 Kings are the historical account of the most important events during the time of the kings of Israel, excluding the first two kings, which are found in the two books of Samuel. This story begins with Solomon, passes through the division between Israel and Judah, and continues until the dissolution of Judah under King Zedekiah. These books point out that idolatry and worship of other gods broke the covenant with God, causing the deportation and slavery of Israel and Judah.

God's people became divided and ended up back to where they started during the time of Moses, on the other side of the Jordan begging for a new opportunity. The author kept a record of these events to demonstrate to the captives that repentance was the only way for the Israelites to become a free nation again.

Many of the stories told in these two books are also told in the books of Chronicles (chronicles of the kings) written by Ezra. Both books have basically the same objective: to remind the people of Israel of their history so they could learn from their victories and their failures in an attempt to bring them closer to God once again.

Introductory questions (10 minutes)

After a brief introduction in which you explain in your own words what you have just read, have the students participate by asking some general questions..

1. If you were named king or queen, what would be one of your first mandates?
2- What would be one of your first prohibitions or rules?
3- How would you like to be remembered?

All rulers try to leave a mark in history. Their dynasty is what makes them unique and special. Some leave a mark that history appreciates, while there are others we would prefer to erase from history.

That is also true of the first kings in the Bible. Some were very popular among their people, others have gone down in history without glory, and some contributed to shaping the world as it exists today.

Development (30 minutes)

We can categorize the books of 1 and 2 Kings according to the main characters:

David: King of Israel, he names Solomon as his successor. 1 Kings 1:1-2:10.
Solomon: Son of Bathsheba and David, the third king of Israel, builder of the temple. The wisest man who ever lived. 1 Kings 1:10-11:43.
Rehoboam: Son of Solomon, successor to the throne. His bad decisions led to the division of the kingdom into Israel and Judah; then he reigned over Judah. 1 Kings 11:43-12:24; 14:21-30.
Jeroboam: King of the 10 tribes of Israel. He set up idols and appointed priests who were not Levites. 1 Kings 11:26-14:20.
Judah under **Abijam and Asa.** 1 Kings 15:1-24.
Israel under **Nadab, Baasha, Elah, Zimri, and Omri.** 1 Kings 15:25-16:28.
Israel under **Ahab.** 1 Kings 16:29-19:9.
Elijah and Elisha. 1 Kings 19:9-21; 2K 2:1-25; 2 Kings 4:1-8:15.
Ahab's last years. 1 Kings 20:1-22:40.
Jehoshaphat king of Judah. 1 Kings 22:41-50.
Israel under **Ahaziah and Jehoram.** 1 Kings 22:51; 2 Kings 1:1-18; 8:16-29.
The **Moabites** rebel against Israel. 2 Kings 3:1-27.
From **Jehu** until the fall of Israel. 2 Kings 9:1-17:41.
The king who pleased God: **Hezekiah**. 2 Kings 18:1-20:20.
Isaiah: Prophet who ministered during the reigns of five kings of Judah. 2 Kings 18:13-19:36.
Judah under **Manasseh and Amon**. 2 Kings 21:1-26.
Josiah and the renewal of the covenant. 2 Kings 22:1-23:30.
Jehoahaz, Jehoiachin, and Jehoiakim. 2 Kings 23:31-24:17
Zedekiah in Judah. 2 Kings 24:18-20.
The fall of Jerusalem. 2 Kings 25:1-26.
Liberation of King **Jehoiachin**. 2 Kings 25:27-30.

Exercise: The king asks...

You may have played this game a thousand times, but what's important is that it makes clear the power that the kings had over their people.

Before the class starts, project or write on a poster or whiteboard a list of things that participants must achieve. You can also just make paper copies and hand them out. Make a list of things that they can easily find around them (a green tree leaf, a black stone, the longest hair etc., depending on where you are) and another list with things that are harder to find or require imagination (the shortest verse in the Bible, a live insect, the pastor's middle name, etc.).

Keep in mind that you will only give them 10 minutes. Blow a whistle or set an alarm so students know when the time starts and ends. Whoever has found the most things will be the winner. (Try to come up with a prize.)

Stories of kings, kingdoms, and prophets
Let's start with Solomon.

Solomon: He was the third king of Israel, the son of David and Bathsheba, and the wisest man in history.
Read 1 Kings 3:7-14 and 4:29-34.

What did Solomon ask of God? What would we have asked for in his place? What was God's request to Solomon?

Rehoboam, the son of Solomon, fourth king of Israel. This king listened to his young friends and instead of helping the people, he imposed even more forced labor on them. The people revolted and there was no one to defend Rehoboam, other than the tribe of Judah, just as God had told Solomon. All Israel except the tribe of Judah made Jeroboam king, and Rehoboam took refuge in Jerusalem with the families of Judah and Benjamin. The kingdom of Israel was divided. On one side Israel, and on the other side Judah.

Read 1 Kings 12:1-20.

Why did Rehoboam decide not to listen to those who had experience, instead listening to his cronies? How do we find wise counselors in our lives?
These three kings were followed by many others. In the midst of all the chaos, God always paid attention to the people of Israel by sending them some very special prophets, among whom the following stand out:

Elijah: Elijah never died. He was taken to heaven alive. He performed many signs in the name of God. One of the most spectacular ones was when he prayed and fire fell from heaven, consuming an entire sacrifice (1 Kings 18:19-40). After several adventures, Elijah was taken to heaven without dying (2 Kings 2:6-15).

Elisha: Elijah's successor. Elisha asked God for a double portion of the spirit that burned in Elijah, and God gave it to him (2 Kings 2:1-18).

Elijah and Elisha were prophets who honored God, and that is why God chose to do great wonders through them. God presented Himself to Elijah in a soft murmur, and gave him the confidence and security to not be afraid, win the battle, and defend those who had never betrayed God by worshiping other gods. God could have shown how strong He was through an earth-shattering earthquake or an uncontrollable fire, but He decided to be a soft murmur, because His power is not in what is feared, but in His love and care.

Conclusions (10 minutes)

Forgetting that God is the one who should truly be on the throne is always a bad idea. The rebellion of the kings led to the division of God's people, and to many rivalries.

Solomon started out very well but then he lost his way, and his reluctance to follow God's counsel had consequences for everyone. Perhaps Solomon felt he was too wise, and his example was passed along to subsequent generations.

God sent prophets. Sometimes He spoke in the fire and other times in gentle breezes. His prophets were imperfect, just like the kings, but God had a mission for both of both the prophets and the kings: to get more people to walk close to Him, and for His people to grow in influence.

Many times we lose sight of the fact that our decisions today echo in our future, our families, and in our cities.

Close the class by thanking the Lord for the books of the kings, and encouraging group members to carefully read the stories from the week's meditations.

Give each participant a copy of Readings from the Kings at www.e625.com/lessons.

Lesson 9 › JOB

The name"Job in Hebrew means "the persecuted one." It is believed that Moses could have been the author of this book because he lived in the same city as Job. Or perhaps the author could be Solomon because of the style of writing. That thinking is the reason why this story was placed in its position in the Bible.

Due to various descriptions within the book of Job, it is also believed that Job lived sometime between the story of the Tower of Babel and the emergence of Abraham. The book of Job begins by recounting an argument between God and Satan, something Job did not know about. Job's friends, and even Job in his ignorance, tried to explain his suffering from a rational point of view, until finally Job was able to rest in his faith, in the goodness of God, and in the hope of redemption. God defended Job's trust in Him, and trust in God is the main message of the book. When there are no rational or theological explanations for sorrow, we can always trust God.

Introductory questions (10 minutes)

After a brief introduction in which you explain in your own words what you have just read, have the students participate by asking some general questions.

> 1- If you had to choose to live through any natural disaster, which would you pick? Why?
> 2- If you had to choose a physical impediment to have for the rest of your life, which one would you choose and why?

We are not always aware of our blessings and opportunities. For many of us, walking or running are easy, going through a natural tragedy like an earthquake or a flood seems unlikely, and we take for granted that when we turn on the tap, clean drinking water will come out. So, when a tragedy happens, it seems like it's the end of the world. It's only then that we realize the value of what we had before.

The story of Job is a tragic succession of misfortunes. By studying this book, perhaps we'll learn to live with gratitude even during the most difficult moments.

Development (35 minutes)

The structure of the book of Job is as follows:
1. The dilemma, God's wisdom, and the debate with Satan (1:1-2:13).
2. The complaint (2:11-3:26).
3. The debates of Job with his friends (4:1-37:24).

- First cycle (4:1-14:22).
- Second cycle (15:1-21:34).
- Third cycle (22:1-32).
- Job's final complaint (29:1-31:40).
4. Elihu's speeches (32:1-37:24).
5. God's intervention (38:1-42:17

Throughout the book of Job there are debates between Job and three friends. At the end, a fourth friend intervenes. To better understand this book, we are going to divide into groups and discuss Job's situation.

The four stations of Job

Choose four spaces in the room with one leader assigned to each space (four leaders total), and divide the students into four groups. Assign the leaders their verses and give them a sheet of paper with a list of questions to guide the conversation. Assign a group of students to each station and a rotation order so they can rotate until each of the four groups have passed through each of the four stations.

Warn them that they will have five minutes per station to read and answer the questions. Set a timer to stay on track.

Station 1: The debate between God and Satan, 1:1-12.
What was Job's life like at first?
What virtues did God highlight in Job?
How did Satan justify Job's behavior?
Why would God decide to test Job's faithfulness?

Station 2: Job's misfortunes, 1:13-22.
Job lost everything he had. If Job's story happened today, what things would he have lost?
What was Job's reaction?

Station 3: Job's second test, 2:1-10.
How did Satan test Job next?
How did Job's wife react?
How did Job react?

Station 4: Two of Job's friends (before class you can choose the verses that you think are best for your audience).

Words of Eliphaz: 4:7-9; 15:1-6; 22:22-30.

What does his friend Eliphaz accuse him of?

Words of Elihu: 32:12; 33:8-19, 29-30; 34:10-12; 35:8; 36:15-16.

What is Elihu's advice?

Have the entire group return to their place and ask them the following question, telling them to remain silent and not answer out loud.

Why would a good God allow His children to suffer?

And after a few seconds tell them:

Because suffering has the potential to bring out the best in us.

Ask them to meditate on that idea in silence for a few moments.

God's response
Now read aloud Job 38:1-3 and 40:1-7.

God asked Job a lot of questions just to show how great he is and how small we humans are.

Conclusions (10 minutes)
Some things we experience are a consequence of our sins. Others are a consequence of the sins of others. Still others are opportunities God gives us to discover virtues in our character that only trials can bring to light.

God knows every sorrowful moment of our lives, He knows everything we lack and everything we need, and no adverse circumstance is a "punishment" from God. He does not repay our bad with something worse. He always blesses us, even through circumstances that are difficult for us to navigate.

Job wisely said, "Shall we accept good from God, and not trouble?" (2:10). God never promised that we will not have any sorrow. We live in a broken world and sorrow is everywhere. It also has the positive side effect of making us sensitive to the suffering of others.

Often we suffer because there are too many people who live in darkness, far from

God, making selfish decisions. We all suffer the consequences of those decisions. It is precisely in suffering that God reveals to us His comfort and His grace. 2 Corinthians 1:2-7 also teaches us this truth (read it). Sometimes we, like Job, don't know why we suffer. Job's friends tried to find the reasons why this had happened, but God simply used what happened to bring out the best in Job. God's faithfulness goes beyond all human perception, and His desire for us is always for good.

Finish by reading Job 42:12-16 and close with prayer.

Give each participant a copy of Readings from Job at www.e625.com/lessons.

Lesson 10 > PSALMS (Part 1)

The Psalms constitute the ancient "book of hymns of Israel," and the name, both in Hebrew and Greek, includes in its meaning the use of rhythm and music.

The psalms were inspired by God to bring human beings into honest worship. We can highlight at least seven authors of the psalms, among them King David, who wrote 75 of the 150 psalms; the sons of Korah, who wrote 10; and Asaph, who composed 12. Other authors were Solomon (two), Moses (one), Heman (one), and Ethan (one). The other 48 psalms remain anonymous.

The psalms were collected over a period of about 900 years of Jewish history. They have always been greatly significant, helping the Jews remember their history and beliefs in an easy and practical way, passing on truths from generation to generation.

Introductory questions (10 minutes)

After a brief introduction in which you explain in your own words what you have just read, you can share these questions to get the students to participate in the conversation.

1- Who likes music, and who is taking lessons to learn an instrument?
2- What type of music do you like the most? Who is your favorite artist and why?
3- What worship songs we sing together are your favorites? Why?

If we think about nature, about the animals, and then we dive into the seas, or fly to the sky, or if we think about the human body, with each part fulfilling a specific function, or even start thinking about the galaxy and the entire universe and how it's all synchronized, we can't help but recognize the miracles and wonders of God. King David knew how to perceive that truth, and he also knew how to express his gratitude to God in a special way. In the book of Psalms we find many songs and poems that exalt God for His works and for His care..

Development (30 minutes)

The psalms present a wide range of theology applied to daily life events. The topics are too varied to relate all of them, but they can be broadly classified as follows:

1. Psalms of wisdom: instructions for leading a wise life.
2. Psalms of lamentation: meditating on sorrows.

3. Psalms of royalty: meditations on the sovereignty of God.
4. Psalms of penance: meditations on the consequence of sin.
5. Psalms of thanksgiving: praise to God.

Psalms can be divided into five sections, or shorter books:

1. Book I: Psalms 1-41.
2. Book II: Psalms 42-72.
3. Book III: Psalms 73-89.
4. Book IV: Psalms 90-106.
5. Book V: Psalms 107-150.

And in general terms, two themes stand out:

Praise: strength, moments of joy, and exaltation of God.
Fragility: weakness, moments of sorrow, and the search for the Lord.

War of Songs

Divide the group in two with equal numbers of women and men in each group, or divide the teams into women versus men. Flip a coin to choose which team starts.

This team must sing a song, and stop at any time they want. The opposing team will have 20 seconds to start another song that begins with the letter or the word the previous team finished with. When one team cannot find a song to follow they lose, and the other team receives a point. Keep playing for 15 minutes. Don't be upset or angry if they use songs that are not Christian, as long as they don't choose anything rude or disparaging.

Book review

Music is, without a doubt, one of the main attractions in young people's world. Many young people bond over their musical taste, dress like their favorite bands, and even start friendships and relationships by sharing with each other the music they like.

The purpose of the psalms was to worship God by remembering His works, and today by reading them we are inspired to think about Him and about what He has done for us. Singing the psalms in modern songs helps us to remember who God is.

Give each participant a copy of In Tune, downloaded at www.e625.com/lessons.

My Worship Psalm

There are many things we talk to our heavenly Father about. When we have a sad moment, when we are happy, or when a situation overwhelms us. But let's be honest, most of the time we come to God when we are going through a situation in which we need Him. Many of us find it difficult to approach God just to thank Him, to exalt His name, to say nice things to God. Human beings feel all sorts of different feelings. Let's use some of them to express gratitude to God.

Pass out a piece of paper and a pencil to each student. Each one must write a psalm of praise. The challenge is that you can only praise God and can't ask Him for anything.

If anyone dares to rap, sing, or recite their psalm, give them the opportunity to do so. If they want to share their psalm with you or with a friend in private, give them the opportunity.

Conclusions (5 minutes)

The book of Psalms makes it clear that praise brings joy to God's heart and to ours, and that there are times to grieve and to be brutally honest about our feelings. God loves to be praised, not because He desires the flattery but because He yearns for our love. He loves it when His children approach Him with beautiful words and with gratitude, because this is good for us. Our earthly songs and praises are a rehearsal for the glorious time we'll spend in heaven praising Him face-to-face, full of total gratitude.

Poetry and art are expressions of God's creativity in us. Praise and worship spring from and express the depths of our being.

Our songs and our praises should arise naturally from hearts full of gratitude and from actions reflecting that gratitude. God wants us to praise Him in spirit and in truth (John 4:23-24).

Give each participant a copy of Readings from Psalms Part 1 at www.e625.com/lessons.

Lesson 11 > PSALMS (Part 2)

Just as the psalms of praise express joy and gratitude, the psalms of frailty show us that fear and anxiety are also feelings God appreciates when they rise as a cry to Him to rescue us. After all, those feelings can be signs of dependency on Him, and God appreciates coming to His children when we have these types of emotions.

Introductory questions (10 minutes)

After a brief introduction in which you explain in your own words what you have just read, you can share these questions to get the students to participate in the conversation.

1- What things used to scare you when you were little?
2- What do you think is worse, being afraid of something or of someone? Why?
3- When something is scary, what is the best way to overcome it?

All of us sometimes feel fear and anxiety. We may not be afraid of things that might jump out the dark or have phobias of spiders or rats, but we may fear being rejected by someone important to us, losing a job or starting a new one, or failing something at school. The psalms teach us about those inner fears that haunt and weaken us.

Development (30 minutes)

Give your students blank papers and ask them to make three columns: Things, People, Feelings.

Note: "Things" means things like natural disasters, illnesses, accidents, lack of something material they need. "People" means someone in particular that they feel some fear or anxiousness around—a boyfriend/girlfriend, a teacher, a boss, a peer, a father or mother. "Feelings" might include loneliness, depression, sorrow, failure, anxiety.

Ask them to write their fear in the column with which they identify it. They may write more than one thing in more than one column.

Now ask them to circle those that they think they can control and put a square around those they cannot control. Ask if anyone wants to share their answers.

Do not be afraid

Give each of your students a copy of "Do not be afraid," which you will find at **www.e625.com/lesson**, and let them respond for a few minutes. There you will also find the teacher's guide.

Reflection on fears, anguish, and the psalms of frailty.

As we saw in the book of Job, we often do not know why certain things happen. Sometimes we might know they are consequences of bad decisions, and/or of the sin of people around us. We live in a broken world and we need God's guidance to live well and enjoy it. But like Israel, we distance ourselves from God too often, focusing on ourselves and our wants. Isaiah 53:6-7 is the prophecy about the cross of Jesus. It says that we all abandoned Him, that each one of us went our own way, but even so Jehovah bore on Him the sin of all of us.

Christ suffered in silence, unjustly, feeling the pain of our abandonment and of bearing all the evil of the world. Jesus knows well what it's like to feel distressed and abandoned, which is to suffer the consequences of sin and evil. But unlike us, He chose to do this to free us from pain, to rescue us, and to reconcile us again with our heavenly Father.

As we saw in the previous class, the book of Psalms takes us to the world of poetry to help us express ourselves on another level toward God in gratitude and praise. But the psalms also lead us to reflect, to pour our hearts out before Him with repentance and sorrow for having failed or anguish over situations we are going through. The psalms of David and other warriors are psalms of praise, of cries for help in times of anguish and of praise even in the midst of anguish. God is not afraid of being asked, "Where are you? Why did you abandon me?" Even Jesus asked Him that question when He was on the cross. God wants you to seek Him when you are happy and also when you are sad. He wants you to rejoice in knowing that He will respond even when you are discouraged. Praising Him while trusting that He will respond to us at the right time encourages us, lifts our spirit, and gives us hope and peace.

Conclusions (10 minutes)

Find one or two popular songs that speak of God's love and His faithfulness in times of distress and fear. If your worship team or someone with a guitar can play these live, even better. If not, you can search for music online (make sure you have a good connection and audio loud enough to drown out any other sounds).

Invite the students to praise the Lord with their hearts, presenting their sorrow, pain, and fears to Him, but with thanksgiving, recognizing that He is faithful and that His power can free us from all evil.

Then close with prayer and ask those who want prayer for a specific situation the opportunity to raise their hand. While everyone sings you can pray with those who raised their hand one by one. Invite some leaders or parents to join you to help you pray with them.

Give each participant a copy of Readings from Psalms part 2 at www.e625.com/lessons.

Lesson 12 › PROVERBS

The book of Proverbs is made up of 513 important reflections King Solomon wrote. It is believed that those 513 were part of more than 3,000 he wrote in total, along with other proverbs written by some other authors who were influenced by Solomon. (1 Kings 4:32; Ecclesiastes 12:9). This amazing book is a collection of comparisons, metaphors, and assertions based on common images and behaviors, while at the same time reflecting the deepest truths of life.

Each proverb is a simple but profound truth that teaches fundamental morality and good judgment for everyday life, reflecting on theological themes at the level of practical justice. Proverbs lead to reflection, questioning our way of thinking, living and managing life in the light of truth.

The two main and contrasting themes of the book of Proverbs are wisdom and folly.

Introductory questions (10 minutes)

After a brief introduction in which you explain in your own words what you have just read, you can share these questions to get the students to participate in the conversation.

> 1- Who are the most important people in your life? Why?
> 2- What kinds of secrets would you share with those people?
> 3- In which situations would you ask those people for advice? Why?

We often talk with our parents or grandparents about things we are embarrassed to talk about with friends, and we talk with friends about things that we think our parents would not understand. But the most important people are always the ones we trust with our secrets and to whom we go for advice. As we grow, we learn to be better sons and daughters, better grandchildren, better friends, etc., and over time we also acquire the wisdom to give advice to others.

Development (30 minutes)

We can categorize proverbs as follows:

Man's relationship with God:
Trust: Pr. 22:19.
Humility: Pr. 3:34.
Fear of God: Pr. 1:7.
Justice: Pr. 10:25.

Sin: Pr. 28:13.
Obedience: Pr. 6:23.
Rewards: Pr. 12:28.
Tests: Pr. 17:3.
Blessing: Pr. 10:22.
Death: Pr. 15:11.

Man's relationship with himself:
Identity: Pr. 20:11.
Wisdom: Pr. 1:5.
Foolishness: Pr. 26:10-11.
Conversation: Pr. 18:21.
Self-control: Pr. 6:9-11.
Goodness: Pr. 3:3.
Wealth: Pr. 11:4.
Pride: Pr. 27:1.
Anger: Pr. 29:11.
Sloth: Pr. 13:4.

Man's relationship with others:
Love: Pr. 8:17.
Friends: Pr. 17:17.
Enemies: Pr. 19:27.
Truthfulness: Pr. 23:23.
Gossip: Pr. 20:19.
As a father: Pr. 20:7; 31:2-9.
As a mother: Pr. 31:10-31.
As son/daughter: Pr. 3:1-3.
When educating: Pr. 4:1-4.
When disciplining: Pr. 22:6.

Medicine for our relationships

On a blackboard, wall, or even on the floor, divide the three categories of proverbs. Print the verses with their quotes on separate sheets of paper, one copy for each team. See the complete table with the correct answers at **www.e625.com/lessons.**

Divide the group as follows: In advance of your time together, cut squares of paper, or any other shape, of three (or more) different colors. Before the students arrive, stick them under each chair. Ask your students to all sit on the chairs, and then have them look underneath to see what color paper is stuck there. Then they must join those who got the same color, forming three teams (or more).

This will be a race. Give them or show them the chart with just the names of the three categories of proverbs. You will need one for each group and all the verses with their quotes. At the signal they must read the proverbs and characterize the verses according to whether it is a proverb that talks about the relationship of God with man, of man with himself, or of man with other people (see example). The team that gets the most correct answers is the winner (you can time them). Whoever finishes first gets 10 points, and they also get 1 point for each correct answer.

Note: The word "man" is a generic word for "human."

Example:

Man with God	Man with himself	Man with others
Pr. 3:34: "He [The Lord] mocks proud mockers, but shows favor to the humble and oppressed."	Pr. 20:11: "Even small children are known by their actions, so is their conduct really pure and upright?"	Pr. 17:17: "A friend loves at all times, and a brother is born for a time of adversity."

Relevant questions

1- What are the verses in the first category about? Why do we say they have to do with our relationship with God?

2- What about the verses in column 2, the ones that contain advice for ourselves? How do they help us become better?

3- Why did we classify the proverbs in column 3 as relevant for interpersonal relationships? How can these tips help us with our relationships?

Proverbs have been important throughout history because they are sayings that are both memorable and loaded with wisdom. All proverbs are excellent to memorize and repeat every day. After all, they were written by Solomon, of whom the Bible says, "I will give you wisdom such as no one has had before or will have after" (1 Kings 3:12).

Conclusions (5 minutes)

Any reasonable person would want to be considered wise.

To fear the Lord does not mean we should be afraid of Him, but that we should give Him the same place in our hearts that He already has in the universe. It is wise to listen to Him, because we can be certain that He has the truth and the keys to lead a wise and good life.

God is the source of all wisdom and He Himself provides the key to obtaining it. God invites His children to be intelligent and able to think for ourselves.

The ultimate goal of proverbs is to help us choose well and thus live life to the fullest.

To finish, read Proverbs 3:1-8 and close in prayer.

Give each participant a copy of Readings from Proverbs at www.e625.com/lessons.

Lesson 13 › ECCLESIASTES AND SONG OF SONGS

Today we will analyze two other books written by Solomon. The name Ecclesiastes derives from the Greek word "ekklesia," which translates to "assembly" or "congregation" and refers to the people. In Hebrew, the name is "Qohelet," which literally translates as "one who collects" "wise sayings" or "one who addresses the assembly." Hence the name "the preacher" or "the teacher," which you can find in some translations of the Bible.

Along with Ruth, Song of Songs, Esther, and Lamentations, this book is part of the group of books called Megillot, "five scrolls" that were read during special occasions.

Ecclesiastes was read at Pentecost, and Solomon probably wrote it during his last years.

The key word in this book is "vanity." The purpose of this book is to warn younger generations not to make the same mistakes Solomon made. Despite being the wisest man in the world, Solomon wasted God's blessing and pursued personal pleasure instead of honoring the one who had blessed him with wisdom. Solomon went from glory to disgrace through vanity. This word "vanity" is used 37 times in the book, expressing that earthly goals and ambitions are inconsequential. Solomon teaches us through his experience that the only satisfying life is one that recognizes God's sovereignty and serves Him. He affirms that the highest good is found in obeying God and fully enjoying life in Him.

The Song of Songs is also known as "The Song of Solomon," indicating that this song is the best of the 5,005 musical works of Solomon. The Jews read this scroll at Passover, calling it "the holiest place."

Song of Songs exalts the purity of marital affection and romance. The main themes in this book are the love of God expressing itself in the love between man and woman, and the grace of God through marriage.

Introductory questions (10 minutes)

After a brief introduction in which you explain in your own words what we have just explained, share these questions to get the students to participate in the conversation.

1- What do you consider more important: money, being loved by other people,

or having an exceptional talent for something? Why?
2- If you could choose to be a genius in any subject, which one would it be?
Why?
3- What would you do if you had access to all the money you can imagine?

Everyone wants to be happy and works hard to be happy, according to what they think that means. Some think that having a lot of money will make them happy, others think that being important or having unique achievements will make them happy. Others think having a large family, many friends, or being famous will give them happiness. But the truth is that there are countless cases of people who have won the lottery and ended up much worse off than they were before they won. We know of artists who seem to have it all but end up taking their own lives, either on purpose or through an accidental overdose. Happiness is about more than any of this. We need something more. The books of Ecclesiastes and Song of Songs are about the truly important things in life, the desires in our hearts, and achieving God's purpose in creating us and thus being truly happy.

Development (35 minutes)

We can categorize the book of Ecclesiastes as follows:

1- Introduction: 1:1-3.
2 - Development of the theme: 1:4-2:17.
- For life in general: 1:4-11.
- For knowledge: 1:12-18.
- For pleasure: 2:1-11.
- For wisdom and folly: 2:12-17.
3 - Research on work and reward: 2:18-6:9.
- Human activity: 2:18-26.
- Time: 3:1-4:6.
- Vain accumulation: 4:7-16.
- All can be lost: 5:1-6:9.
4 - Solomon's conclusions: 6:10-8:17..
- Lack of knowledge: 6:10-12.
- Prosperity and adversity: 7:1-14.
- Justice and impiety: 7:15-24.
- Women and foolishness: 7:25-29.
- The wise man and the king: 8:1-17.
5 - Words of advice: 9:1-12:14.
- Wisdom and foolishness: 9:1-10:15
- The government of kings: 10:16-20.
- Excessive caution: 11:1-8

- Enjoyment of life: 11:9-12:8.
- Final advice: 12:9-14.

And we can categorize Song of Songs as follows:

1 - Courtship: 1:2-3:5.
2 - The wedding: 3:6-5:1.
3 - Marriage: 5:2-8:14:14.

Ecclesiastes and Song of Solomon have the same author, and he also wrote the book of Proverbs. If you remember the previous lessons, Solomon was the king and the wisest man in the world. The book of Ecclesiastes is like an intimate diary in which Solomon shared his deepest feelings after having already gone through many life experiences. He had studied so much, he had achieved so many things, he had experienced everything he could have experienced, he had traveled to many places, but none of it made sense to him anymore. He felt that everything was absurd and that nothing in this world had value or meaning unless it was enjoyed under the plan for which God had created him.

Artwork with wisdom

Divide your group into four small ones. If you need to divide into more groups you can adapt the following instructions. To create groups, put colored pencils in a bag, in equal numbers depending on the number of students you have. If you don't have colored pencils, you can use colored straws.

Give each team a piece of cardboard or a long strip of white paper and different drawing elements such as colored pencils, paints, brushes, crayons, markers, anything you can get (I know that sometimes it is difficult to have these materials, but there are always parents willing to collaborate, families with children who discarded them, schools that do not need them, etc.).

Then give your students one of the cards that you will find at www.e625.com/lessons with the name of this activity

Ask them to make a piece of art that represents that passage. Then they have to explain it to the larger group. Tell them they don't need to create a single drawing or a single concept. They can draw parts, they can do work together or individually, but they should try to represent as much as they can on the paper.

Ecclesiastes carries warnings from Solomon. It's as if a father, a grandfather, or perhaps an older brother is warning us not to put our hearts and energies into things that pass away, that do not last, that lose their flavor, or that do not lead to anything better. Ecclesiastes teaches us that everything has its time, that we do not need to worry, that hoarding without sharing has no reward, and that our character or inner self is more important than anything we can find on earth. Solomon also leaves us with a great piece of advice for young people. Read Ecclesiastes 11:9-12:8. Why would someone who had lived through so much and who had experienced life's greatest pleasures recommend this to us? Let your group share their thoughts.

Profound love

In addition to the book of Ecclesiastes, Solomon wrote Song of Songs, poems about perfect love. Like a work of art, this book shares scenes of passion between two lovers both before and after getting married. Although there are some somewhat personal descriptions included, Solomon compares this love story with the love of God toward His church, a profound, true, and pure love. God IS love. One of the ways to express a couple's love is through romantic love, where attraction and passion are key. God created this too; He put all those feelings into us as humans. God knows what we feel and has established the right time and person for it. It is important to first understand the values Solomon teaches us in Ecclesiastes, learning what is truly important, before we fully and purely enjoy true love, like God's love for us.

Compliments

What street compliments do you know, things people might shout to a stranger on the street? How do they make you feel?

Think of some popular compliments popular in your city to repeat if your students don't remember or don't know any.

Divide the group into women on one side and men on the other, and appoint one person from each group as the guide or leader for this activity.

Have the leader divide these passages among the women, and have them read them as a group:
Song of Solomon 1:15; 2:14-15; 4:1-15; 6:2-4; 7:1-9
Have the leader divides the following verses among the men:
Song of Solomon 1:12-14; 2:3-6; 5:10-16; 7:10-13; 8:6-7

How are these love verses similar to the verses we hear today?
How do they feel about each other?
Which part most caught your attention and why?

Conclusions (10 minutes)

God does not want us to prioritize accumulating things. Everything has its place. His advice is good and those who obey Him prosper.

He is our creator. He formed our bodies and our feelings, and He wants us to do well both in work and in love. In other words, He wants us to be wise in public and in private, in the assembly (Ecclesiastes) or in the home (Song of Songs).

Satan is the father of lies. He wants to ruin our lives, both in public and in private. This is why it is good to analyze the message of Ecclesiastes and Song of Songs. A wise person will learn to differentiate vanity from what is wise, and will also learn to practice love in private.

Just as Ecclesiastes teaches us to differentiate what is important from what is superficial, Song of Songs reflects the character of God. Just as the ideal husband loves his wife, God is faithful (8:5), God is loving (8:6), and God is pure (3:5; 4:1,16).

May Solomon's advice be engraved in our hearts so that we can enjoy life in abundance.

Give each participant a copy of Readings from Ecclesiastes and Song of Songs, downloadable at www.e625.com/lessons.

Lesson 14 > OBADIAH AND JOEL

Obadiah means "servant of Jehovah." Obadiah's prophecy refers to a historical event in which the Edomites allied themselves with the enemies of Israel and participated in the sacking of Jerusalem. In Genesis 25:19-27:41, we have the story of the twins Jacob and Esau. Jacob traded Esau's birthright (although they were twins, Esau was born first) for a bowl of lentils. Thus Jacob was left with the best blessing and inheritance from his father. From Jacob the people of Israel were born and from Esau the people of Edom were born. Esau later forgave Jacob, but Edom was always at war with Israel. While God told Israel that they must never return evil for evil because Edom was family, Edom took advantage of every opportunity to ally itself with the enemies of Israel and plunder their cities. God was not pleased with Edom's actions, and His judgment fell on Them. As Obadiah predicted in verses 10 and 18, the people of Edom disappeared from the face of the earth.

The prophet Joel focused his message on Judea and Jerusalem. His name means "Jehovah is God." Although the prophet showed that he knew in detail the temple and its uses, he was not a Levite but belonged to the tribe of Reuben. Joel 3:4-6, 19 refers to the same events that are also described in the book of Obadiah. The prophet Joel compared their suffering from a locust invasion to the image of an army, suggesting that it was a foreshadowing of "the Day of the Lord," the period of the Lord's wrath and judgment, the day when God would reveal His character. Joel called everyone to repentance, promising that if they were faithful, their land would be restored. The attitude of a man's heart and their life before the Lord will determine God's reaction on the day of His judgment. Those who call on the name of the Lord will be saved.

Introductory questions (10 minutes)

After a brief introduction in which you explain in your own words what we have just explained, share these questions to get the students to participate in the conversation.

1. Which social injustices bother you the most?
2. What punishment would you give to someone who commits that injustice?
3. How would you compensate a victim of injustice?

The books we are studying today deal with prophecies given by Joel and Obadiah on behalf of the Lord regarding injustice. In their prophecies, the Lord was angry. He ceased to protect Israel for having distanced itself from Him. But upon their turning to God, He would punish those who were harming Israel.

God protects and then compensates the victims, just as we, or any good movie hero, would do.

Development (30 minutes)

Structure of the shortest book of the Bible:

God's Judgment against Edom: 1:1-14
Judgment against all nations: 1:15-16
Restoration of Israel: 1:17-21

Structure of the book of Joel:

1- The day of the Lord: 1:2-2:17
      The locust invasion: 1:2-12
      First call to repentance: 1:13-20
      Second call to repentance: 2:12-17
2- Avoid judgment and receive blessings: 2:18-3:21
      Introduction: 2:18-21
      Material restoration: 2:21-27
      Spiritual restoration: 2:28-32
      The coming judgment: 3:1-16
      National restoration: 3:17-21

Images to delete

Look for images of social injustice: children in extreme poverty, beaten women, people sleeping on the street, images of racism, police fighting against civilians, abandoned elderly, mothers with children begging in the streets, people sorting through the garbage looking for food, men lining up to get work, etc. Print them and present them to your young people and ask them these questions:

      Which of these images impacts you the most and why?
      What do you think can be done about it?
      Have you ever seen or experienced this?
      What can we do about it?

Review of the books

Prophets were people who communicated messages from God to His people. Most of the time, prophecies did not relay good news. Usually, God's purpose with these messages was to restore His relationship with his people, make peace, and help them find happiness with Him.

The book of Joel first compares the devastation the people had suffered from a plague of locusts with an army that would fall on Israel (ch. 1).

Then he calls them to call upon the Lord and tells them how terrible the devastation will be without God (ch. 2). The Lord promises them many more blessings when they turn to Him wholeheartedly.

In chapter 3 he promises them that when the day of restoration comes, the enemies who attacked and devastated them will be judged by the Lord; judgment will fall along with the divine promise that the nation of Israel will never again be invaded by foreigners.

In verses 4 to 6 of this chapter, Joel addresses exactly what the ENTIRE book is about: Obadiah's vision. In Genesis 25:19-27:41 we are told the story of the twins Jacob and Esau. Jacob traded Esau's birthright for a bowl of lentils (although they were twins, Esau was born first).

So, Jacob was left with the best blessing and the inheritance from his father. From Jacob the nation of Israel was born and from Esau the nation of Edom was born. Although Esau forgave Jacob (Gen. 33), Edom was always at war with Israel. God told Israel that they should never repay Edom evil for evil because they were family, but Edom took advantage of every opportunity to ally itself with the enemies of Israel and plunder their cities.

Joel 3:5 states,You have taken my silver and gold and all my precious treasures, and have carried them off to your pagan temples." God was not pleased with this and brought His judgment on Edom. Joel 3:19 says, "But Egypt will become a wasteland and Edom will become a wilderness, because they attacked the people of Judah and killed innocent people in their land." As Obadiah predicted in verses 10 and 18, the nation of Edom disappeared from the face of the earth.

Joel 3:21 says of God, *"Shall I leave their innocent blood unavenged? No, I will no."* God unleashed His anger against Edom and other nations.

God did not abandon those who had suffered the devastation of the attack of other armies. In addition to giving those who attacked and robbed them what they deserved, He also rewarded and restored those who were victims of the attack and were taken as slaves. He also returned their lands and wealth. See Obadiah v. 19-21 and Joel 3:18.

The Lord is attentive to those who love Him, surrender to Him, and adopt Him as Lord. He wants to be our protector, He wants to be our refuge, and He wants to fill us with blessings. Loving Him means following Him, following Him means obeying Him, and obeying Him means remaining under His protection, because His commandments are full of love.

He who loves does not harm. When He corrects us, He does it to bless us. That's how God wants to be with us. *"The Lord will roar from Zion and thunder from Jerusalem; the earth and the heavens will tremble. But the Lord will be a refuge for his people, a stronghold for the people of Israel. Then you will know that I, the Lord your God, dwell in Zion, my holy hill. Jerusalem will be holy; never again will foreigners invade her"* (Joel 3:16-17).

Conclusions (10 minutes)

Give your young people paper and pencils. Ask them to write down a situation in which they were treated unfairly or in which they were victims of something that they could not control.

Tell them that at the end of the meeting, if they wish, they can give their paper to a trusted person within the group, or they can tear it up.

Close by affirming that God is just, that God loves them, that He will defend them just as He defended Israel, and that they can be part of the mission of representing this just God in the lives of other people.

Close with a prayer proclaiming victory over injustices and asking God for wisdom and courage like the prophets had, to speak about the injustices and to do something about them.

Give each participant a copy of Readings from Obadiah and Joel, downloadable at www.e625.com/lessons.

Lesson 15 > AMOS AND MICAH

Amos means "bearer of burdens." This prophet was a fig gatherer. Amos, like Hosea (Hosea 1:1), was called to deliver his message to the northern tribes of Israel during a time of moral corruption. Amos speaks of two main themes: the absence of true worship of God and the lack of justice. Just like Hosea, Amos highlights the infidelity of the people of Israel. He presents a series of judgments from God against the nations, condemnation, and then restoration.

Micah's name is a play on words that means "Who is a God like you?" Micah was a contemporary prophet of Isaiah. Like Isaiah, his message was for Judah. While Isaiah prophesied in the castles, because he had easy access to the king, Micah prophesied outside Jerusalem, on the border of Judah and Philistia near Gath. Like the prophet Amos, Micah lived in a rural, agricultural area, far away from politics and religion. Micah condemned social injustices and religious corruption, the same issues Amos had warned Israel about some years before. When Samaria fell, thousands of refugees arrived in Judah, bringing their gods and rituals, causing the disintegration of individual and social moral values, which Micah incisively addressed. In this lesson we will study the prophet Amos and his message to the northern kingdom, Israel, as well as the prophet Micah addressing the same message to the southern region, Judah, a few years later.

Introductory questions to the topic (10 minutes)

After a brief introduction in which you explain in your own words what you have just read, have the students participate by asking some general questions.

1 - What is your favorite pastime when you are alone?
2 - What things are fun only when you are with a group of friends?
3 - Have you ever done something that you never thought you would, just to fit in with a group of friends?

People often do really foolish things when we mix with the wrong people. It is not uncommon for a good person to get into trouble with so-called friends who seem to have a great time doing evil or making fun of others. This is not a foreign topic in the Bible. Micah was prophesying against the inhabitants of Judea. God's people had mixed with people from neighboring cities and had adopted many of their customs, spiritual rituals, and gods. God wanted to prevent all this. Amos also rebukes the people for having distanced themselves from God, for having made false gods, and for loving evil.

Development (30 minutes)

The book of Amos can be categorized as follows:

1. Judgment against the nations: 1:1-2:16
2. Condemnation against Israel: 3:1-6:14
3. Visions of judgment and restoration: 7:1-9.15

The book of Micah can be categorized as follows:
1. God judges Israel and Judah and promises freedom: 1:1-2:13
2. God judges rulers and promises freedom: 3:1-5:15
3. God judges and redeems: 6:1-7:14

Problems in Israel and Judah

Have some of your students read the following verses aloud and then ask: What are the people's problems or sins? What does the prophet accuse them of?

Amos 4:1
Amos 5:10-12
Micah 2:1-2
Micah 3:9-11

Oppression of the helpless, mistreatment of the needy, injustice, lies, excessive taxes, bribery, selling at unfairly high prices, deceiving people, making evil plans, raising house rentals, violence, etc. God's people, both in Israel and Judah, were going through difficult times; both groups had distanced themselves from God. And as a consequence they were doing horrible things against the most needy among them.

Sometimes when we get together with the wrong people, we do things we know we shouldn't. Sometimes we commit injustices, mockery, or evil, forgetting who we are and who our God is.

Have students write on a blank piece of paper if a situation they were involved in comes to mind as you read the following list. (As your students write, commend this moment to the Lord and ask Him to clearly reveal to them what they've done due to peer pressure.)

It could be an act like offending someone, an act of vandalism such as stealing or destroying someone's property, or it could be viewing pornography, horror, or violence, taking drugs, alcohol, tobacco, or engaging in other addictive or harmful behavior. Start reading from the following list while your students listen.

. If you have ever acted unjustly against someone, mocked their inferior status, mistreated a classmate or sibling, if you forgot who you are and offended the Lord, tell Him.

. If you have ever done something because your friends were doing it, because they were watching, even though you knew it was against your morals, this is the time to confess it.

. If you have ever stolen, broken something belonging to someone else on purpose, if you have cheated on someone to look good with your friends or to gain someone's favor, you can write it now.

. If you have adopted a way of dressing, speaking, or behaving just because others do it, but you know that it does not fit with your moral values and that it dishonors God, you can choose to surrender this to the Lord.

. If you have ever cut yourself, hurt yourself, or done something against your body to feel included in a group or for any other reason, you can confess it now, on this paper.

. If you have ever participated in inappropriate games, sexual or demonic, if you have made oaths and promises that should only be made to God, you can write it now as a confession to the Lord.

Ask if anyone wants to share their experience. Everyone should listen respectfully. If a student chooses to share, immediately pray for that student.

When they finish writing...
God knows everything we wrote on our papers. We cannot hide anything from Him. He knows our feelings too, and He knows why we did what we did. But He does not persecute us for our mistakes. God chose to love us and He expects us to realize our mistakes, big or small, and to confess them to Him because keeping them "secret" keeps us apart from Him.

Micah 7:18 says: *"Who is a God like you, who pardons sin and forgives the transgression of the remnant of his inheritance? You do not stay angry forever but delight to show mercy."*

God's greatest pleasure is to love.

Conclusions (10 minutes)
Ask the student to listen to the reading of the following two passages, and then to respond together to the teacher's guide you can download at **www.e625.com/lessons.**

Amos 5:14-15: *"Seek good and not evil, that you may live; so the LORD God of hosts will be with you, as you have spoken. Hate evil, love good."*

Micah 6:8: *"He has shown you, O mortal, what is good, and what does the Lord require of you? To act justly and to love mercy and to walk humbly with your God."*

Close by giving thanks for God's forgiveness.

Give each participant a copy of Readings from Amos and Micah, downloadable at www.e625.com/lessons.

Lesson 16 > ISAIAH

The name Isaiah means, "Jehovah is salvation." Isaiah was the prophet in charge during the reign of four monarchs of Judah: Uzziah, Jotham, Ahaz, and Hezekiah.

Isaiah belonged to an influential family with access to the king. He was raised in Jerusalem and had knowledge of politics and religion, which distinguished him from the other prophets, who were simpler men. Historically, Isaiah has been compared to other great thinkers, not only because of his message but because of the extraordinary way in which he wrote. He focused his message on Judah. He condemned idolatry and, even though his message was one of warning, he also prophesied more about hope than any other prophet.

Isaiah provided information about Israel's future on earth. He is the prophet mentioned the most in the New Testament, and his word carries great weight due to the large number of his prophecies that have already been fulfilled. Isaiah is also known as "the evangelical prophet," as he spoke a lot about the grace of God, especially in his last 27 chapters. Chapter 53 is the key. In this chapter he paints a portrait of Christ as the slain Lamb of God. In this lesson we are going to highlight one of the book's central themes, holiness, as seen in chapter 6.

Introductory questions to the topic (10 minutes)

After a brief introduction in which you explain in your own words what you have just read, have the students participate by asking the following questions.

> 1- How would you describe your idea of God in a few words?
> 2- In what ways do we serve the Lord?
> 3- Who are the people who know God the best?

Many times we have preconceived notions about who God is. We might believe our conception is correct, but God is not the same for everyone. We might also limit ourselves to believing that only certain roles within the church truly serve the Lord, or believe that those who know the most about God must be those who teach or speak on His behalf. The book of Isaiah contains many prophecies from God about various nations, not just Israel and Judah. There are promises, condemnations, and restoration. Chapter 6 is very interesting, because in it, Isaiah presents God in a new and incredible way.

Development (35 minutes)

We can categorize the book of Isaiah as follows:

1- The judgment 1:1-35:10
- a- Judah and Jerusalem: 1:1-12:6
- b- Judgment of the nations: 13:1-23:18
- c- Redemption of Israel: 24:1-27:13
    - 1- Devastation of the land: 24:1-23
    - 2- Songs of gratitude: 25:1-26:19
    - 3- Discipline of Israel: 26:20-27:13
    - 4- Warnings against Egypt: 28:1-35:10

2- Historical account: 36:1-39:
- a- Sennacherib: 36:1-37:38
- b- Hezekiah: 38:1-22
- c- Babylonians: 39:1-8

3- Salvation: 40:1-66:24
- a- Release from captivity: 40:1-48:22
- b- The Servant's sufferings: 49:1-57:21
- c- Future glory of Zion: 58:1-66:24

Recognizing the old

Gather some everyday objects such as kitchen utensils, office supplies, things that can be found in a bathroom, etc. Ask several volunteers to come forward, cover their eyes, and pass these objects around so they can guess what they are. To make it more interesting, set the timer for one minute and see how many items they can get right. The player with the most correct answers will be the winner.

Without sight, even simple, everyday objects can seem confusing. Most of us are so used to seeing everyday items that we take them for granted, but when we encounter them in a different way they take on a whole different meaning.

Main ideas

Isaiah went through a similar experience. Isaiah was bringing words of condemnation to the kings and princes of different kingdoms. He was fighting against hypocrisy, injustice, and oppression, and because of that, his life was constantly at risk.
He knew what it was like to be unpopular and experience the consequences of communicating God's truth to powerful people. Isaiah knew God and had heard and obeyed God's voice, and yet we can see in chapter 6 that even Isaiah had to learn to truly know God. Although he had served Him many times, the Lord still had much to show Isaiah.

Read Isaiah 6:1-8 carefully. What can we highlight from this passage? Write the clues on a blackboard or another visible place:

1- High and exalted Lord: The original says YHVH. Here Isaiah refers to God that way out of reverence, so as not to pronounce the name of God. YHVH means "God is." Isaiah implies that he is seeing the one who is God, and highlighting God's greatness.

2- The seraphim: They indicate purity, yet they are not pure enough to see the glory of God, so they cover themselves in God's presence.

3- They sing: "Holy, Holy, Holy." Saying holy three times indicates that He is infinitely holy. It is because of this infinite holiness that everything trembles.

4- Isaiah is extremely **fearful:** He knows he is nothing in the presence of the Holy One. Although he was already a prophet prior to this passage, recognized as exceptional, and though he would have more prophecies fulfilled than any other prophet in the Bible, in contrast to God he is impure.

5- One of the seraphim flies to Isaiah and **purifies** his lips. The seraphim declares Isaiah sinless, making him holy. Does this sound familiar to you? We are all holy because of the forgiveness of our sins, and that gives us access to God's presence. But before this can happen, we need to declare ourselves impure.

6- "Whom shall I send? And who will go for us?" Wasn't Isaiah already serving the Lord? Many of us can likely relate to Isaiah. We are satisfied with some role we are fulfilling, and we believe we are doing a good job. Even so, it is still necessary to be in communion with God. The best life comes when we know His plans, which are always better than what we imagine.

7- "Here I am, **send me!"** Isaiah does not hesitate; he wants to be someone who makes a difference. Could we say no to such an invitation?

Give each student a copy of the worksheet: "Between God and I" that you can download at **www.e625.com/lessons.** Give your group a few minutes to respond in writing, or have them respond in pairs or in groups of 3-4 people each.

Conclusions (10 minutes)

God always has a better plan than the one we come up with for ourselves. When we find ourselves in His presence and He reveals Himself to us in His sublime essence and infinite holiness, we have nothing left to do but to recognize who we are to

Him. It doesn't matter if you are a young man trying to find your path in life or the most recognized prophet in the Bible, the pastor with the largest church, or a relative nobody with few friends. God is God and He is infinitely holy, and before this holiness, we are all sinners. Until we recognize our condition before God, God cannot sanctify us.

God wants to make us holy not so that we can be "well behaved" or be seen as good people, but so that we can enjoy His presence, and so that He can use us in powerful ways. That is why we need Jesus Christ, who through His death cleanses and sanctifies us so we can have a relationship with the Father.

Sometimes it is scary for us to think that God has a plan for us. Perhaps that is why He asks Himself, "Whom shall I send?" But if we trust in His promises and in His majestic power, He will show us a future to which we cannot help but say, "Send me."

End in prayer acknowledging that we need to be purified to enjoy God's presence so that He can communicate to us His plan for our lives.

Give each participant a copy of Readings from Isaiah, downloadable at www.e625.com/lessons.

Lesson 17 > NAHUM, HABAKKUK, AND ZEPHANIAH

The importance of the prophets does not lie in who they are themselves but in their message, and that is why we do not have much personal information about some of them. These three prophets made prophecies related to the power of Assyria and its capital, the great city of Nineveh—the same city that a century earlier had been confronted by God through Jonah. Once again Nineveh was full of evil. Their bloodthirsty armies laid waste to entire populations, and piled the people's bodies like mountains to display a spectacle of power.

Introduction questions to the topic (10 minutes)

After a brief introduction in which you explain in your own words what you have just read, have the students participate by asking some general questions.

Anyone who has a position of power, whether at work, at school, in a family, or in a church, can take advantage of that power or authority.

1- Have you had a situation where someone with authority abused their power, like a teacher, a boss, a manager, etc.?
2- How did it make you feel to not be able to defend yourself or report it?
3- Have you taken revenge for that injustice? Did anyone defend you? Did what had happened even come to light?

At some point in our lives all of us are going to experience abuse of authority. That authority may despise us, may make us feel inferior, or may commit a great injustice to us or to others.

In these three books, the people of Israel were being mistreated, taxed, killed, and enslaved. The enemy—the Assyrians—were incredibly cruel. The Assyrians had their capital in the city of Nineveh. They not only killed all the people who opposed them, but they boasted of their cruelty and mutilated their enemies' bodies, piling them up. They were bloodthirsty and they enjoyed what they were doing. God would not allow the situation to remain that way. Through these prophets we see the destruction of Nineveh prophesied, and we can see the process of waiting for God's justice and victory.

Development (30 minutes)

Nahum. He was the one who first predicted the fall of Nineveh due to its evil, describing how the overflowing of the Tigris River would destroy the walls of

Nineveh. He further prophesied the city's demise (3:11), which occurred after the Babylonian attack in 612 BC. The destruction was so complete that the remains of the city were not found until 1842 AD.

The outline of themes in Nahum could be:
    1- Nineveh is judged: 1:2-15
    2- Nineveh is destroyed: 2:1-13
    3- Nineveh and its misfortune: 3:1-19

Ask your students to open their Bibles to the book of Nahum.

What are the titles of these passages?

Depending on the version that they use different words will be highlighted, but generally they will be: Destruction of Nineveh, Liberation, Victory over Nineveh, Fall of Nineveh, the end of Nineveh, Total Destruction. God had become angry with the violence and repression of Nineveh and He had a plan. God's justice was imminent, and although His people had gotten into this situation because they had been unfaithful, God is always faithful. The people suffered consequences, but heavenly help was on the way

Reflection:
Have you gone through serious situations as a result of a bad decision you made?
Did you come to that decision with or without God's guidance?
How did you get out of it?

Now let's go to the book of Habakkuk.

Habakkuk starts with a complaint to God for how long it was taking Him to avenge the injustice of the Assyrians' violence. God gave Habakkuk a vision and told him to write in detail the end of Nineveh for all its sins and bloodthirsty behavior. His prophecy includes the attack of the Babylonians that would destroy the city. We could divide the book of Habakkuk as follows:

    1- Presentation: 1:1
    2- First complaint and first response: 1:2-11
    3- Second complaint and second response: 1:12- 2:20
    4- Habakkuk's prayer: 3:1-19

What does Habakkuk say in chapter 1:2-4 and 1:14 and 17? Have you ever found yourself in such a situation?

How does God respond in 2:2 and 3?

How would you explain Habakkuk 3:17-19 in your own words?

And finally we'll study the prophet Zephaniah:

Zephaniah prophesied during the reign of King Josiah. After Assyria lost power and control of the region, Nineveh's rule weakened. For the first time in 50 years Judah tasted independence, at least for a while. Thanks to Zephaniah's influence (who was of noble blood) through his prophecies, and from having found the book of the law, King Josiah began to do good before God and brought great reforms to the government. It was during the government of this king that Zephaniah prophesied against several nations and peoples neighboring Judah. He also stated the fate that would befall Nineveh, just as Nahum and Habakkuk had done.

Zephaniah's outline could be::
    1- Reflection: 1:1
    2- The judgment of the Lord on the nations: 1:2-3:8
    3- The blessing of the Lord on the nations: 3:9-200

Zephaniah was only 16 years old when they found the book of God's law, and thus he regained the faith of his ancestor David. With it he began a reform in his culture, demolishing the pagan gods and sanctuaries. At 23, he renovated the temple of Solomon.

Finally, a prophet çwho was heard. Although the king was very young, the Lord desired to use his power to restore relationships and complete God's judgment on the nations that oppressed them.

Read Zephaniah 3:16-20
What is God's promise?
Why does God defend His people and make those promises?
How does this ending make you feel?

Conclusions (10 minutes)

The Lord defends His own.

God knows all our sufferings, He knows when we experience injustice, and He is not going to let things stay that way. Nahum 1:7 says, "The Lord is good, a refuge in times of trouble. He cares for those who trust in him."

For the same reason, it is important for us to always be compassionate with our brothers. He is their Lord too, and He is jealous of each of his children. No one mocks God and therefore no one mocks us, because we are His children. He is the refuge and protector of those who trust in Him, and that means that we must never be indifferent to His will. We must take it into account in each of our decisions, both to avoid suffering bad consequences, and to be protected by Him in difficult situations.

Close in prayer thanking Him for being our refuge.

Give each participant a copy of Readings from Nahum, Habakkuk, and Zephaniah downloadable at www.e625.com/lessons.

Lesson 18 > EZEKIEL AND DANIEL

Ezekiel means "God's fortress." Ezekiel received his call to prophesy at a very young age. The message he had to communicate to the people of Israel—who were then captives in Babylon with him—was simple but terrible. His task was to warn them of the coming catastrophe and affirm that this was God's plan for His people because of their own rebellion. The city of Jerusalem and Jehovah's temple would be destroyed, but God would forgive those who repented and kept His commandments.

Daniel means "God is my judge." Daniel was a young man after God's heart. He faced pressure and terrible threats against his life and the lives of his friends, yet Daniel always chose to follow God. He was an Israelite who was captive in Babylon, and God called him to prophesy about the things He would do because of the Israelites' rebellion. Daniel's God-given abilities enabled him to serve as an advisor to King Nebuchadnezzar. He was a contemporary of Ezekiel.

Introductory questions to the topic (10 minutes)

After a brief introduction in which you explain in your own words what you have just read, have the students participate by sharing these questions.:

> 1- When you get to work or sit in a college class, what is the worst thing that can happen?
> 2- What things do your parents (or other adults) repeat over and over, as if you're a baby?
> 3- What news could someone tell you when you wake up that would make you happy for the rest of the day?

Ezekiel and Daniel were very young when God called them to be prophets. They lived at the same time and place, and were taken into captivity by the king of Babylon along with many other Israelites. Both had important roles and were responsible for communicating what God wanted to tell His people: to stop their rebellious behavior, repent, and know that God wanted the best for them. Each had a specific message. Ezekiel's message was for the people, and Daniel's was for Nebuchadnezzar, the king of Babylon.

Development (35 minutes)

We could categorize the book of Ezekiel as follows:
1- Prophecies about the ruin of Jerusalem: 1:1-24:27

       a- Call of Ezekiel: 1:1-3:27
       b- Condemnation of Jerusalem: 4:1-24:27
2- Prophecies against the nations: 25:1-32:32
3- Repentance of Israel: 33:1-33
4- Restoration of Israel: 34:1-48:35

Daniel's outline would be:
1- From Jerusalem to Babylon: 1:1-21
2- Daniel's dreams: 2:1-7:28
3- Daniel's prophecies: 8:1-12:13

Phrases that stir us on the inside

Make cards with messages related to your students biggest and least big interests. For this you will need to know your group. The messages below can serve as examples.

Have a volunteer read the messages, and instruct the group to agree on the score for each phrase (one point would be for the worst phrase, the one they do not want to hear, and five points for the best phrase, the one they do want to hear).

Here are some examples, but you should come up with more according to what you know about your students:

"We're doing inventory at work today."
"Last minute exam."
"Next week you are going on a trip to Europe."
"I have a surprise for you."
"Fasten your seat belt."
"Pick up the clothes off the floor."
"Who wants ice cream?"
"Budget meeting tomorrow morning."
"Well done, excellent job."
"We are going to visit your grandparents."
"We have not received your payment."

Questions for discussion:

What happens when we hear things that we don't like much?
How do these phrases affect our lives?

Review of the books

Ezekiel and Israel

At that time these books describe, the Israelites were stubborn and did things as they saw fit, without consulting or taking God into account: they lived in continuous sin and for that reason they became prisoners of war in Babylon.

When God spoke to Ezekiel, He warned Ezekiel that the people were not going to want to listen to him because they were stubborn. Still, He asked Ezekiel not to remain silent but to speak to them anyway. It would be up to the people to decide whether or not to listen to God's message (Ezekiel 2:1-9; 3:7-10).

God then spoke to Ezekiel again, asking him to ask the people of Israel to turn from their evil behavior and experience a better life, because He loved them deeply. If the Israelites continued being stubborn in their thinking they would surely die, and that is why God asked Ezekiel to speak to them so that they would repent. Read Ezekiel 3:16-19 and respond:

How do we react when we see someone do inappropriate things?
Is it easier to stay silent or speak God's truth?
Have you ever been in a situation in which you had to warn someone that what they were doing would have bad consequences, while knowing that they did not want to hear what you had to say?
Have you ever been the one who didn't want to listen to someone's warning?

Another young man who had to speak up and not remain silent was Daniel.

Daniel and the king

Daniel became an advisor to King Nebuchadnezzar, a position he obtained because God had given him the ability to interpret dreams. King Nebuchadnezzar had a dream and did not understand its meaning, which worried him. He sought among his wise counselors and none of them could interpret his dream. They recommended that he seek the advice of Daniel (Dan. 2:1-3).

Daniel believed in God and trusted Him. He knew that his life would be in danger if he did not interpret the king's dream. Daniel asked God to help him interpret the dream, and God did. God listened to Daniel and gave him the interpretation, and Daniel went to tell King Nebuchadnezzar. Let's read Daniel 2:36-49 together.

In Daniel chapter 3 the king had a large statue made of his image so that everyone in Babylon would worship him. The only ones who did not worship the king's statue were Daniel and his friends, who were wise and God-fearing. The king became angry and sent them to a great furnace to burn them. But God sent an angel to take care of Daniel and his friends, and they came out alive! The king then worshiped God (Daniel 3:19-28)!

Both Daniel and Ezekiel were courageous in the place in which God placed them. Daniel influenced three kings during his lifetime. Ezekiel focused his whole life on leading the Jews to repent and return to God.

What stops us from sharing Jesus with others?
Write on a whiteboard, or somewhere visible, the responses your group members give to this question. Share a personal situation in which you experienced any of the feelings they mention, and how you worked through it.

Also share ways that they can talk with others about Jesus and His work on the cross.

Conclusions (10 minutes)

Christians have an important message to share: Christ's message of love and salvation. God loved people so much that He sent His son Jesus to die for us so that all who believe in him may have eternal life (John 3:16). This message is unique and powerful and all people— friends, family, schoolmates, everyone—need to hear it. When Christ is the center in our lives, everything makes sense. Sometimes we will find ourselves in situations where we'll have to say, like Daniel, "I am not going to defile myself!" When this happens, the Lord will support us like he supported Daniel and his friends.

It will not always be easy to talk about God, His love, and the things He has taught us through his Word. Sometimes we are afraid of being seen in a bad light or of being mocked or made to suffer. In all circumstances, God is right there where we need Him. We must have the faith and confidence to give our lives for Jesus' cause. Didn't He give up his life for us?

Finish by reading Matthew 5:14-16 and then pray that God will give your students what they lack and enable them to carry on His message. Encourage them to share Jesus with their friends during the week and to invite others to join them at church next time.

Remember that you are an example. Share with your neighbors, co-workers, and family members about the Lord, and tell your students about those experiences next time.

Give each participant a copy of Readings from Ezekiel and Daniel, downloadable at www.e625.com/lessons.

Lesson 19 > JEREMIAH AND LAMENTATIONS

The books of Jeremiah and Lamentations are cries to God over the misfortunes that befell the Hebrews as a result of their not repenting and instead worshiping idols, dishonoring God.

Joshua had prophesied many years earlier about the destruction of Jerusalem (Joshua 23:15-16), and Jeremiah was mocked for predicting the same (Jeremiah 1-35). Yet, when the judgment was fulfilled through King Nebuchadnezzar and the capture of Judah to Babylon, Jeremiah responded with great pain, sorrow, and suffering.

Jeremiah was a priest and prophet who became known as "the weeping prophet." He had a life of great suffering, and often compared Israel's suffering to his own. His message was primarily for Judah, although occasionally he prophesied against other nations. Jeremiah left with a remnant of Jews who fled to Egypt and was taken captive by King Jehoiachin when he invaded Egypt. The main themes of Jeremiah are the judgment on Judah and the restoration of the future messianic kingdom.

As for the book of Lamentations, it is believed that its author was Jeremiah, because of some indications of parallel language with the book of Jeremiah, such as in Jeremiah 7:29 and 2 Chronicles 35:25.

Lamentations was translated from the Greek "ekah" or "loud cries." As its name suggests, the book contains lamentations that recall the suffering caused by the fall of Jerusalem under the power of Nebuchadnezzar. This book keeps alive the memory of past glories and teaches how to face suffering.

Introductory questions (10 minutes)

After a brief introduction in which you explain in your own words what you have just read, have the students participate by sharing some questions.:

1- Have you ever felt very sad? What was the reason?
2- Have you had a close friend or family go through something difficult that caused them to be sad for a long time?
3- What was the best way to get over sadness?

Some things are difficult to go through: the loss of a loved one, the breakup of a relationship, losing a job, being denied a promotion, failing an important test, parents' divorce. These are things that produce deep sorrow that lasts for a long time.

We can see this kind of sorrow in the two books we are going to study today. One is the book of Jeremiah. Jeremiah was a priest and prophet who went through much pain and suffering. He wrote about the suffering of the people of Israel who were under the rule of other kings and nations. The people were slaves and suffered all kinds of sorrows, punishment, forced labor, hunger, and abuse from those who dominated them. The other book is Lamentations, and the author is believed to have been Jeremiah. Lamentations expresses this same sorrow.

The Bible was written a long time ago, but we can see from its pages that people have been enduring difficult times for as long as humans have existed. Today we will see how we can get through those times, move forward, and rise from deep sorrow to eternal joy.

Development (30 minutes)
We could organize the book of Jeremiah as follows:
1- Jeremiah's Call: 1:1-19
2- Messages to Judah: 2:1-45:5
       a- Judgments of Israel: 2:1-29:32
       b- Restoration of Israel: 30:1-33:26
       c- The fall of Judah: 34:1-45
3- Judgments on the nations: 46:1-51:64
4- The fall of Jerusalem: 52:1-344

We can divide the book of Lamentations as follows:
1- First Lament: The suffering of Jerusalem: 1:1-22
2- Second Lament: The wrath of the Lord: 2:1-22
3- Third Lament: The suffering of Jeremiah: 3:1-66
4- Fourth Lament: The suffering of Zion and punishment of Edom: 4:1-22
5- Fifth Lament: Prayer for mercy: 5:1-22

Challenges and dares
Each player will draw one card from the pile that you will prepare beforehand. If you have many participants, just ask for a few volunteers. After reading what the card says out loud, they will respond with one of two things: They can say "No problem!" and complete the challenge, or they can say "I have a problem on my hands" and choose someone else to do what the card says instead of them. The person they choose may or may not also reject the challenge. If they fulfill it, they "save" both players. If they reject it, the first player must draw another card with another challenge—but the condition is that they must complete the second challenge, even if it's worse than the first one. They cannot go back to the previous card. Give everyone who completes the challenge a small reward, like candy.

Print the "Challenges and dares" page at e625.com/lessons, cut out the squares to use as cards, and put them in a sack or bag or lay them out face down..

After the game, ask the following questions:
1- Why is it that what's a problem for some people is not a problem for others?
2- Do you think that there are people who have more problems than others? What do these people tend to have in common, if anything?as?

Problems vs. Hope
1- Jeremiah began by prophesying the calamity that would come upon God's people if they did not repent of worshiping other gods and turn away from evil. Jeremiah had a problem on his hands: He had to give the people bad news as a warning. (Jeremiah 7:1-11.)

2- Not only did he have to give a warning message that the people did not want to hear, but Jeremiah himself would suffer the consequences of his own warnings. The prophet had a big problem on his hands. (Jeremiah 20:1-2; 37:13-16; 38:4-6.)

3- Israel had a big problem on their hands: They had distanced themselves from God and now they were suffering the consequences of their bad decisions. As Jeremiah had prophesied, Babylon would take Judah captive and they would suffer as slaves, but they did not listen to him and now it was too late. Open the Bible to Lamentations, and let the students find verses that affirm what was said.

4- The Lord always has a plan (Jeremiah 46:27-28; 50:4-7, 33-34). God would rebuild in the future everything that had been left in ruins. He keeps His promises and always seeks the well-being of those He loves.

Conclusions (10 minutes)

In these two books everything that's being shared is terrible. The infidelity on the part of the people brings sorrow to God. This fills Jeremiah with sorrow. He suffers from having to prophesy what would later take place, and he also suffers from seeing the people of Israel suffer during their years of captivity, slavery, and abuse by Babylon.

The entire book of Lamentations contains complaints, crying, and suffering from all three parties. This shows us that it is valid to feel sad and to cry and mourn for what is lost, for what is not gained, or for what we suffer. This is all part of living and growing.

But that does not mean we should or will remain in that sad state. We will suffer many consequences, but we must learn from them, becoming wiser so we can live better. We will become better able to trust in the Lord and in His word, and to understand why it is good to obey Him. Obedience is God's love language, and He is always close to those who seek Him and obey Him. Our hope is in His promises. Read Romans 5:1-5.

Does God promise anywhere in the Bible that we will never have problems if we are Christians? No. So, what does the Lord promise us?

God promises us that He will be with us in the midst of problems and that the Holy Spirit will comfort us and guide us with wisdom if we are willing to obey. Read Romans 15:13.

Close in prayer by asking your students what things to ask of the Holy Spirit, such as to guide you to find comfort, hope, and the wisdom to make intelligent and mature decisions that will lead to fullness in Jesus.

Give each participant a copy of Readings from Jeremiah and Lamentations, downloadable at www.e625.com/lessons.

Lesson 20 > HAGGAI AND ZECHARIAH

Because of the hardness of the people's hearts, God sent them a strong wake-up call: the Babylonian captivity. Despite false prophecies that predicted that this would be a short period of captivity, God announced that it would last 70 years. He promised that He would then bring the people back to their land. In fact, on the precise date, under the authority of a new empire, the people received the freedom to return home. An edict by Cyrus of Persia allowed a group of the exiles to return, led by Zerubbabel (governor and political leader) and Joshua (High Priest and religious leader). The first mission they had to complete was the reconstruction of the temple.

Introductory questions (10 minutes)

After a brief introduction in which you explain in your own words what you have just read, have the students participate by asking some general questions.

Have you experienced a serious wake-up call from God?

Why do you think rebuilding the temple was an immediate priority?

What do you think your reaction would be if God had fulfilled His promise of restoration and then gave you a new opportunity to fulfill your mission?

Development (30 minutes)

Upon returning to Jerusalem, the leaders and the people began rebuilding the temple. However, intimidation and bribery led to discouragement and their abandonment of the project. Fifteen long years had passed since the setting of the foundations of the temple. Haggai's message was the first thing the people heard from God since their return home from exile.

Depending on the size of the group, divide them into teams to facilitate conversation. Assign each team to work on either Haggai or Zechariah (it doesn't matter if multiple teams work on the same book; the important thing is to give them the opportunity to discuss their observations and encourage each other with the implications for today). Teams will then be able to share some of their thoughts with the group.

Haggai: a look inward

Read chapter 1 of Haggai. At that time, the people were in a serious crisis. Mention the verses and specific phrases that denote the economic crisis of the town. Do the same again, but highlighting the spiritual crisis. For us today, do you think there would be a correlation between an economic crisis and a spiritual crisis? In this particular case, we see that the external (economic) crisis was caused by God so that the people would have a reaction to their internal (spiritual) crisis. Could God do the same in our lives today?

What words would you use to describe the attitude of the people toward the mission they had to complete? Refer to examples from the Scripture you read. The people's problem was not a problem of lack of information, but of lack of submission. As a team, come up with a list of at least 10 biblical instructions we know with certainty are our purpose in life. Why do you think it is so difficult for us to obey on matters that we know so clearly God wants us to do? How important is it for each of us to fulfill God's mission, versus fulfilling our own will? Which of "your own things" might be preventing you from doing "God's things" today?

In the passage we notice an important note of hope. God gives the people an opportunity to exercise obedience to Him. The people humbly repent and start doing God's will. What would it take for us to change our behavior so radically?

Does God still give us those types of opportunities today? What could you do this week to take action regarding your mission on this earth? What evidence would demonstrate your spiritual priorities?

Zechariah: a look into the future

This book contains two large sections: chapters 1 to 8, about the visions at night, and chapters 9 to 14, with the prophecies of God's judgment and the coming kingdom. Many of the texts in this book are extremely difficult to understand (surely not even Zechariah himself understood them!), and some of them only make sense later, after Jesus appears on the scene.

Read 1:1-6. We find an urgent call for the people to turn to the Lord. This is always a matter of the heart, but it manifests itself in external negligence (outward conduct). In what ways is the abandonment of the construction of the temple evidence of the heart of the people? What happens when we ignore our mission in our daily lives? What does that say about our hearts? Zechariah refers to the sins of the people's ancestors. How can we learn from those who came before us, generations of people who either abandoned or fulfilled God's purpose for their lives?

The section from 1:7 to 6:8 contains eight visions in which Zechariah is wide awake and asking questions. Distribute the prophecies among team members, or select some to be read individually, and discuss them. What does this prophecy say about the restoration of Jerusalem (Zion)? What does it say about the Messiah who will come? What does it say about the role of the people before other nations, their relationships and testimony?

Discuss how these prophecies provide a look into the future as well as encouragement to fulfill the present mission.

Read 8:1-23. This prophecy is given two years after the first eight visions. God promises joy and restoration. Meanwhile, the temple must be rebuilt! How encouraged should we be when we see that God will do the impossible? In this passage, what other practical implication does hope for a glorious future have for the present? How is that behavior a reflection of the people's mission?

Conclusions (10 minutes)

Prophets were messengers who spoke with conviction on God's behalf, delivering His message. Many prophecies announced future truths as well as present implications. These books continue to show us God's faithfulness in dealing with His people and fulfilling His covenant with them. They give us hope while challenging us to live out the mission the Lord has entrusted to us.

To finish, take time within your teams to pray for each other and write some phrases that represent a prophetic message for the entire group. This does not mean coming up with mystical messages or divining specific aspects of someone's future. Instead, write sentences that you know to be true based on your reading of the biblical text. Sentences that bring encouragement to the group, that challenge you all to live in obedience, and to fulfill the mission. What is God telling us today? They may be statements similar to those of Haggai: "God says that if we obey and work on what He has asked us to, He promises us His presence and His blessing." Encourage one another by sharing these prophecies out loud.

Give each participant a copy of Readings from Haggai and Zechariah, downloadable at www.e625.com/lessons.

Lesson 21 > ESTHER

There are only two books in the Bible named after women and both are found in the Old Testament. We will now study the second one.

The book of Esther is interesting in that nowhere does it directly mention God. Yet God's presence is implied, and there is no doubt that He intervened supernaturally in everything that happened with Esther. Esther is a beautiful book that the Jews read during Passover to remember God's hand of mercy on His people.

Introductory questions (10 minutes)

After a brief introduction in which you explain in your own words what you have just read, have the students participate by asking some general questions..

1- Have you or a family member ever gone through a difficult season that required a lot of prayer and faith?
2- In that time, what people came close to you and accompanied you?
3- Have you ever interceded for someone going through a difficult time? How did you get involved and how did you feel about it?

Development (30 minutes)

EThe book of Esther tells the story of a beautiful young woman who became queen of Persia. Although she was Jewish, King Ahasuerus (father of Artaxerxes, the king who let Nehemiah go to Jerusalem to rebuild the wall) fell in love with Esther's beauty and character, and named her queen instead of Queen Vashti (who, because she refused to go to the king's party, was stripped of the title of queen). God definitely had a plan for Esther: She was going to be Israel's defender during a time of calamity.

Haman, one of the most important officials in Persia, hated Mordecai, who had raised Esther. Even though by decree everyone had to prostrate themselves before Haman, Mordecai would not do so; he remained standing. Haman had sworn to kill Mordecai, and not just him, but all the Jews. Haman had an extermination plan ready to put into action. Queen Esther heard about it and asked her people to fast and pray for her while she also fasted and prayed. Then she interceded with the king for her people, even though her life was in danger.

It's important to know that in difficult times we can count on people who are willing to accompany us and cry out to God for our needs. It's an honor to be able to intercede for those who need our help in their most difficult moments. But the most precious thing is knowing that God puts us in the right place to be there for each other in the most complicated moments.

A great story of courage and mission.
Divide the students into teams. Do this by supplying photos of as many beauty products as the number of groups you want to make: lipstick, wrinkle cream, tweezers, etc. Print as many copies of each image as the number of participants you want per group. Place the pictures in a bag and have each person choose one without looking. Students will be grouped with those who've picked the same image.

In their teams, have students read Esther 3:5-11, 4:11, 4:15-17, 7:1-6, 7: 9-10, 8:16. (It would be best if they divide their tasks, but let them figure it out for themselves.)

Fast and furious!
Draw a line on the floor with chalk, or with tape. The leader will ask questions about the story of Esther and one player per team must run to the line, step on it, and give the answer. Ask one or two volunteers to be line judges to determine who steps on the line first. The first player will have the opportunity to answer. If they answer correctly they get a point. If they answer incorrectly, the player who came in second will get the chance to answer. Get the questions with the correct answers at www. e625.com/lessons

If there is a tie, break it with a more complicated question, like what does verse 4:14 say in your own words? Let them look for it, read it, and respond.n.

Conclusions (10 minutes)

At times we will face difficult situations that will test our faith, our obedience, and our trust in the Lord. In times like these it is important to have the support of the church, to help us remain faithful to the Lord. It's important to know that we can count on the prayers, fasting, and spiritual support of our brothers and sisters, and that they can count on us to do everything necessary to fulfill the purpose the Lord has entrusted to us.

The Lord is not mentioned in the story of Esther, but Esther obviously trusted Him, which is why she asked the people to pray and fast with her. Two points to highlight:

- • Esther understood that she was there to serve her people.
- • She knew she could count on their spiritual support.

This is a good opportunity to spend time praying for your students' prayer requests.

Ask them to stand in pairs or groups of three, share their prayer requests, and pray for each other.

Also prepare a mailbox with paper and pencils so that they can place private requests they don't want to share with the group. (Tell them this once they have finished praying, so they can first have a time of trust and not keep all requests private.)

Give each participant a copy of Readings from Esther, downloadable at www.e625.com/lessons.

Lesson 22 > EZRA AND NEHEMIAH

Ezra and Nehemiah tell about the people returning from captivity and rebuilding both the temple and the city. This took a long time, and it happened during a very difficult period. The Jews encountered strong opposition, particularly from the Samaritans, a neighboring people with a mixed Jewish and pagan heritage.

Nehemiah had the challenge of rebuilding the walls of Jerusalem. Ezra had the challenge of teaching God's law and engraving it in the people's hearts.

Introductory questions (10 minutes)

After a brief introduction in which you explain in your own words what you have just read, have the students participate by asking some general questions.

1. 1. Why do we encounter opposition when we desire to live God's purpose for our lives?
2. 2. What kind of attitude allows people to take advantage of new opportunities and start again after a failure?
3. 3. What does it take to overcome obstacles caused by other people and those we cause ourselves?

Development (30 minutes)

The books of Ezra and Nehemiah are very strict when it comes to the purity of the people. Although we see here the physical work of reconstruction, there is a greater emphasis on the inner construction of each individual. What lessons do we learn about this in Ezra 7:10?

Debate

An extremely complex issue for the people during those times, as well as for us today, is that of mixed between followers of Christ and those who do not follow Christ. This is not a simple matter, and it can be a controversial topic. However, it is an important and spiritually relevant issue. With this in mind, prepare the group for a debate.

Divide everyone into two teams and ask both teams to read Ezra 9:1-15 and Nehemiah 13:23-27. Then, they will have time to prepare for a debate. One of the teams will defend mixed relationships (you can focus on courtship and/or marriage) and the other team will be against them. Remind them that this is not a fight against people from the other group but rather a dialogue between two points of view.

Give the groups several minutes to prepare their explanations, and then the debate begins: "Should a Christian be in a dating and/or marriage relationship with someone who is not a Christian?"

The arguments are very likely to include passages like 1 Corinthians 7:16 and 2 Corinthians 6:14. It is worth studying them as part of your preparation.

Moderate the exchange in a way that it remains a healthy debate (again, it's not about attacking or hurting people on the other team). At the end, ask the following questions:

1. What dominated our discussion: existential arguments or biblical arguments? Were the biblical arguments from passages relevant to the topic, or were they taken out of context?
2. Is the topic we debated primarily a social issue or a spiritual issue?
3. If our purpose in life is to make God's character known to others, in what ways does our faithfulness to God strengthen our mission? In what ways does our unfaithfulness weaken it?

Difficult decisions

Take some time to read all of Ezra chapter 10. Highlight the words of verses 2 and 3: "We have been unfaithful to our God, but there is still hope for Israel. Let us make a pact with our God." The three elements are a wonderful reminder of God's character, and ours. His grace is still with us today.

After reading the chapter, how would you rate the steps the people took? What implications did they have on the Israelites and on others?

Some of your group members may be currently involved in mixed relationships. Making decisions about such circumstances will be an individual process. Remember that each case is different and there is no single way to approach them. Be sensitive to the situation and try to understand what your students are experiencing.

Others may be considering starting a new relationship with someone who doesn't believe in God or follows another faith, or they may eventually face a similar situation. Discuss as a group what preventive measures you could prepare for now. How can you support each other spiritually when faced with a possible decision?

Conclusions (10 minutes)

The people's obedience to God's rules was an instrument to let the nations know who their God was and what He was like. Holiness is closely linked to the mission. Throughout the entire story of the Bible, the obedience that God demands and deserves is total, without reservation. That should be our desire. Take time to pray for each other, strengthening yourselves to make decisions based on obedience and as a testimony of your faith in God.

Just like the people during those days, we are incapable of being completely faithful without God's help. Take time to thank and praise God for His grace and mercy and the hope we have in Christ.

Give each participant a copy of Readings from Ezra and Nehemiah, downloadable at www.e625.com/lessons.

Lesson 23 › MALACHI

About 100 years had passed since the people returned from Babylon. The temple had been rebuilt and the sacrifices were being offered again. However, the people had grown tired of waiting for the restoration of Israel. They were living as a small province within the Persian Empire and were in spiritual decline. They had turned away from outward idolatry, but neglected to get rid of the idolatry in their hearts.

Introductory questions (10 minutes)

After a brief introduction in which you explain in your own words what you have just read, have the students participate by asking some general questions.

1. How would you define idolatry?
2. In what ways do you think a Christian could fall prey to idolatry today?
3. How is idolatry connected to spiritual apathy or insensitivity?

Development (30 minutes)

The people were in a state of spiritual decline. They were denigrating God in a terrible way.

Rebuke

Form small groups to read the following passages. They are rebukes, in which the people are being accused of sin. In each case, they contradict the Lord and ask Him for evidence of His accusations

1. Malachi 1:2
2. Malachi 1:6
3. Malachi 1:7
4. Malachi 2:14
5. Malachi 2:17
6. Malachi 3:7
7. Malachi 3:8
8. Malachi 3:13

To better understand each text, it is important to also read the verses that surround it. What do you notice in these rebukes? Why are these important issues? In which ways might they be rebukes for us today?

After listening to the comments from each group, draw everyone's attention to two questions:
1. Why do you think the first rebuke is about insensitivity to God's love?
2. How can we prevent spiritual indifference? How can we prevent our hearts from becoming hard?

Hope
The last words of the Old Testament are recorded in Malachi 4:1-5. Read the passage.

The prophet warns that the day will come when evil will be destroyed. For those who are faithful to God, there will be liberation and well-being. What do you think of the metaphors used in these texts?

Once again there is a wake-up call for the people. They must obey God and they will receive blessing; otherwise, judgment will come. This message from God has been consistent throughout the Old Testament. Do you remember any other situation in which this same promise appears? Is this something God continues to tell us today?

Finally, there is talk of the coming of Elijah. The Jews expected the arrival of this prophet before the coming of the Messiah. Read Matthew 11:11-15. Who does Jesus say John is? Who does John say Jesus is?

Conclusions (10 minutes)

Half-hearted worship is very dangerous. In truth, it is idolatry. Within it, all of us are exposed and vulnerable.

End with a time of prayer and singing. Look for songs that speak to God in the first person and exalt Him as King and Lord. While students sing, prepare a large blackboard or poster board with enough space so each student can spontaneously come up and write specific actions that reflect worship of God. They can be phrases that begin with "I worship you when…" or "I will surrender in adoration to…" More than music, worship is surrender.

Give each participant a copy of Readings from Malachi at www.e625.com/lessons.

Lesson 24 > HOW DO THE OT AND NT COMPLEMENT EACH OTHER?

Someone said that it is unfortunate that we have a page in our Bible that separates the Old Testament from the New, because it seems to create a much bigger break than there should be. Of course, it's not the fault of a piece of paper. However, it is true that the general tendency is to disconnect both sections of the biblical text from each other. We often lose sight of how they complement each other.

Introductory questions (10 minutes)

After a brief introduction in which you explain in your own words what you have just read, have students participate by asking some general questions.

To do this, mark with symbols (or simply with words) two ends of the room in which you are gathered. For example, if you stand in the middle, you can say that your right side will be the first option and your left side will be the second option. Explain to the group that you will read a series of questions, each with two possible answers. Each person must walk and stand at the end of the room that best represents their opinion. When you consider it appropriate, ask some of them why they made their selection.

1. Do you prefer reading the Old Testament or the New Testament?
2. Would you rather be the apostle Paul or Moses?
3. Which is more important, Genesis or Revelation?
4. Which are more difficult to understand: parables or prophecies?
5. Would you like to read and understand Hebrew or Greek?
6. Are the scariest stories found in the NT or the OT?
7. Would you rather see the manna from heaven or the multiplication of the loaves?
8. Where is God presented as more loving, in the OT or the NT?
9. Where is God presented as more just, in the OT or the NT?
10. Would you rather see the sea divided in two or the transfiguration?
11. Do you know more biblical texts by heart from the OT or the NT?
12. Which are you going to read completely this year, the OT or the NT?

You can think of more questions depending on the characteristics of your group. Of course, although we may have our opinions and preferences, there is never competition between the two sections of the Bible. Both are absolutely important, necessary, and sufficient.

Development (30 minutes)
Incomplete definition

Ask the group what the Bible is. If possible, write down their answers. If you want to unsettle them a little, ask them why they give such answers (you will notice that many of the answers are simply memorized answers rather than convictions they have arrived at through intelligent research).

Beyond these initial definitions, many people read the Bible as something it is not. Below is a list of imprecise and incomplete concepts of what the Bible is. When you read them, you will see that the Bible does indeed contain some of these elements, but it is about much more. Share the following categories with the group, and think about well-known biblical examples.

1. The Bible is a book of laws and rules.
2. The Bible is a book of good advice.
3. The Bible is a book of beautiful stories with beautiful lessons.
4. The Bible is a book of promises.
5. The Bible is a book of very famous phrases.

For each case it is easy to recall an example we all know. However, there are other books that contain these same categories that are not called "the Word of God." What is the difference then? And what is the problem?

The big difference

What makes the book we call the Bible (actually a 66-volume library) unique is that it contains God's revelation. A first definition of revelation is "the supernatural manifestation of a truth that was hidden" (De Andrade, Theological Dictionary).

If the biblical text is God's revelation, it means that through it we come to know three truths that would be impossible to know through our own research or experimentation:

1. The character of God (who God is)
2. God's work (God's mission)
3. God's expectation (how God expects us to respond)

Divide the group into teams of 3 or 4 people each, and give them a few minutes to write down some specific reminders about each of these three truths. In other words, after the tour of the Old Testament, what have we learned about God's character, God's work, and God's expectations?

That is the distinctive character of the biblical text! Therefore, every time we read stories, prophecies, parables, advice, proverbs, poems, commandments, or promises, we do so to know God, to learn about His work, and to come to understand how to respond as He deserves and demands. We shouldn't just stop at a law or a story or a piece of advice. We should look at the person it points to. In other words, if we read any portion of the Bible and did not get to know God, His work, and His expectations better, we have read it wrong.

The person of Christ
Of course, in addition to having the written word, we also have the living Word: Christ. He makes known to us God's character, shows us more accurately God's mission, and speaks to us with clarity of God's desire and the response He expects from us. Christ is the revelation of God's revelation.

For this reason, reading the Bible requires us to look toward Christ, both in the Old and the New Testaments. This does not mean we should force the passages to say that Christ is in them, or that all of them refer to Christ. Rather, we should note how the Old Testament announces the Christ who is coming and that the New Testament announces the Christ who already came and now sends us. Therefore, we also read the entire Bible through the lens of God's mission.

Conclusions (10')

Which is more important, the Old or the New Testament? Which one should we pay more attention to?

At this point it would be worth issuing a research challenge to the group. Surely we all have some information regarding the theological and historical themes of the Bible. But many times that information might lack reasoning or understanding. A good project could be to encourage the group to develop a presentation of topics related to the Bible, including:

1. Theological definition of "revelation"
2. Theological definition of "inspiration"
3. Theological definition of "enlightenment"
4. The formation of the Old Testament canon
5. The formation of the New Testament canon
6. The deuterocanonical books
7. The differences between biblical translations and the manuscripts used for each of them

It's not necessary to offer an academic exposition, but the group could benefit from delving beyond the surface into each of these topics. Additionally, the challenge gives you the opportunity to teach your group how to use study tools.
Don't worry about not being able to answer all the questions that arise—instead, worry if questions don't arise!

Help students during the week with their research, and at the next meeting have them share their findings. Let them enjoy the challenge!

Lesson 25 > THE GOSPELS, CHRIST'S INCARNATION

Although the Gospels do not give us the exact date of Jesus' birth, we have some information about it, like the fact that it happened toward the end of Herod's reign (Matt. 2:1; Luke 1:5). Only the Gospels of Matthew and Luke tell of the birth/incarnation of Jesus, the Son of God. We notice several parallel accounts between them: in both Gospels, an angel announced before the birth of Jesus that He was the promised Messiah, of the line of David; Mary was a virgin when she became pregnant through the Holy Spirit; Jesus was born in Bethlehem (David's birthplace) and grew up in Nazareth (Galilee). Both provide the genealogy of Jesus to demonstrate that Jesus is the promised Messiah.

There are also some differences we should be aware of. Matthew's account focuses more on Joseph, while Luke focuses more on Mary. Matthew describes Herod's attempt to kill Jesus and the family's flight to Egypt. Luke draws a parallel between the birth of Jesus and that of John the Baptist. Luke also describes the census decreed by Augustus Caesar that caused Joseph and Mary to arrive in Bethlehem, where Jesus was born, and describes the visit of the shepherds.

If we read John 1:1-18, we find that John identifies Jesus as the Word, who was with God, who is God, who became man/incarnate (the Son of God who voluntarily took a body of flesh and a human nature) to give us life, salvation, draw near us, and be among us (Matt. 1:21-22). Also read John 14:8-11. In it, you will see how Jesus Himself declared His divinity while He was on earth. The Word becoming flesh is the authentic Shekhinah (a term that expresses the visible presence of God in glory). The Jews said, "Where there are two gathered in my name to study the law, the Shekhinah is in their midst," a phrase that Jesus explains in Matthew 18:20. The divine presence is manifested in acts of mercy, of goodness, and of healing those oppressed by the devil (John 1:14; 2:11; 11:4-40; 12:50).

Matthew points out how the Scriptures were fulfilled in the birth of Jesus. God had the plan to rescue and save His creation. The Old Testament is mentioned five times in just the first two chapters of Matthew: Matthew 1:22-23 (Isaiah 7:14); 2:5-6 (Micah 5:2); 2:15 (Hosea 11:1); 2:17-18 (Jeremiah 31:15); 2:23 (Isaiah 11:1). Matthew presents Jesus as the fulfillment of long-awaited hope. Paul in Philippians 2:5-8 explains the incarnation and challenges us to take on the same attitude as Jesus.

Introductory questions (10 minutes)

After a brief introduction in which you explain in your own words what you have just read, have the students participate by asking some general questions.

- What do they say about Jesus in classes at your universities? What do your friends and classmates say about Jesus? Who do they say Jesus is?
- What do you know about the incarnation?
- In the Bible, who was incarnated? How do you know?
- If you asked your friends or classmates, "Is God near or far from us?" what do you think they would say?

Development (30 minutes)

Lead your students to Matthew 1:21-22. Depending on the size of the group, divide them into groups of two or three to read and study the following passages and answer the following questions.

- What names did they need to give this child who would be born?
- Why these names?
- What do these names have to do with the incarnation?
- Why should He take human form with a body of flesh?

To help them a little more with the topics of sin, salvation, and forgiveness, you can give them these passages: Isaiah 9: 1-2; Ephesians 2:1-7; Matthew 1:21; Romans 3:23; 5:12 and 19, 6:23.

- • Who took the initiative to reach out? Matthew 1:22; John 1:14; 1 John 4:19.
- • What is the purpose of Jesus' incarnation?
- • How would we know what God is like and how He works if He had not sent His Son to live among us as a man?

You can give them these passages for reference: John 14:8-11; 1:14; 2:11; 11:4-40; 12:50.

To take things a little further:

Create three groups. Two of them will debate among themselves whether Jesus really is the incarnate Son of God. The third group must evaluate the arguments made by both groups in light of the Word. Give five minutes for each group to organize. Help set the tone for an open and respectful discussion.

Conclusions (10 minutes)

Ask each group to share at least two conclusions and how the incarnation affects them in their daily lives.

- Today we also need forgiveness as we continue to deal with sin and its effects.
- We are not alone, because God came close so we could know Him.
- God always keeps His promises.
- God works in our favor through His mercy and grace, even though we did not deserve His forgiveness and salvation.
- God takes the initiative to get closer, despite our rebellion.

Finish by reading to them Philippians 2:5-10 and Matthew 28:19. Help students understand that we have Good News to announce. We are to take on the same mission Christ did when He became man, making disciples and followers of Him.

Give each participant a copy of Readings from the Gospels: Christ's incarnation, at www.e625.com/lessons.

Lesson 26 > THE GOSPELS, CHRIST'S MINISTRY

The word for "ministry" in Greek is "diakonia" (meaning to serve or assist), and in Hebrew it is "abad" (to serve, labor, enslave, work). Jesus Christ is the perfect example of a servant of God and men.

Read Matt. 20:28, Mark 10:45, Rom. 11:13, 2 Cor. 4:1, and Hebrews 1:17 and 6:4. The Son of God humbled Himself and adopted the status of a slave when He washed men's feet and healed a man's sores. Jesus did not see being a servant as something bad or unworthy. What is unworthy is when a man wants to dominate another man. Read Matthew 20:25 and Mark 10:42.

Two events prepared Jesus to fulfill His messianic role:
1. 1. He submitted to the baptism of John, identifying Himself with the repentant people of God. As He emerged from the water, a voice was heard declaring Him to be the Son of God (Matt. 3:13-17).
2. 2. The Holy Spirit led Him into the wilderness, where Satan tempted Him. By resisting each of Satan's temptations and not giving in by acting for His own good and power, Jesus proved He was ready to fulfill God's purposes and plan as His servant (Matt. 4:1-11).

Introductory questions (10 minutes)

After a brief introduction in which you explain in your own words what you have just read, have the students participate by asking some general questions.
What concept does "the world" want us to have of God?
Do you believe that God works in our favor? Why or why not?
What is your life's purpose? How does your faith impact your sense of purpose?

Development (30 minutes)

Before beginning to read and study the Bible quotes, give each participant a blank sheet of paper and markers or colored pencils. Ask them to draw their life's purpose and what they are doing or will do to achieve it. (I suggest you play music in the background, as this helps create a good environment.) Once they have finished, ask if there is someone who wants to share and explain what they wrote.

Ask students to read Mark 10:42-45 once silently. Now read it aloud once, but in different versions (they will probably have different versions, otherwise ask them to search their mobile devices for at least three or four different versions).

- What word is repeated most often? (servant/to serve)
- According to these verses, what is the importance of serving or being a servant?
- How does the world's concept of service and success contrast with God's concept?
- Take a look at your drawing. Does it reflect more of the world's idea of service, or more of God's?
- According to verse 45, what is the purpose of Jesus' ministry?
- Whose servant is Jesus? Read John 5:30 and 36.
- Whose will or plan was Jesus fulfilling?
- Whose will should we follow? Let's read Matthew 12:50 and 7:21.
- What risk do we run, according to those verses?
- We should not lead inconsistent lives. If we say Jesus is our Lord, that God is our Father, we should act accordingly. Again, look at your sheet and update it if necessary so that it reflects who your Lord is.

We often hear that we should fulfill our own dreams, and that when we seek to involve God in our plans it is so that He may bless them. But according to the verses we have studied, are those ideas based on the Bible? Why? Allow the people in the group to express their opinions. This should help you to better understand where they stand, where their convictions are, what some of their struggles are. Help them to understand biblical truth. If necessary, return to the verses already mentioned and let them look for the answers for themselves.

- Why does God expect us to obey Him—to get involved in His plans rather than following our own?
  Read Luke 9:23-25.
- God's plan has always been to rescue us from sin, to give us life in Him through Jesus Christ. God is not the cosmic party pooper.

Conclusions (10 minutes)

Give each person a new blank page and ask them to draw what their lives would look like under the conditions God has set for us.
- Every action and word that Jesus did or said was to reflect the Father.
    - Do your words, thoughts, and actions reflect God's mercy and grace?
- God is fulfilling His redemptive plan (rescuing us from sin) through the service and ministry of Jesus. Our goal is to be and act just like Jesus.
    - What adjustments must you intentionally make to be a disciple who denies themself, who takes up their cross every day, and follows the Lord?

Give each participant a copy of Readings from The Gospels, Christ's Ministry, at www.e625.com/lessons.

Lesson 27 > THE GOSPELS, CHRIST'S PASSION

Read Luke 22:1-20 carefully, and pray that reading it will impact your whole mind and heart.

The night before He was crucified, Jesus gathered His disciples to have one last supper that, according to the text, He was very much looking forward to. The Passover was a traditional meal every Jew celebrated once a year to remember the miracle of God delivering His ancestors from Egypt. Jesus transformed this ritual into the Lord's Supper, a dinner in which His disciples would eat bread and drink wine to remember their Lord's sacrificial death on the cross.

Now read as if for the first time Luke 22:39-46.

Jesus went to the garden of Gethsemane to pray, preparing for His ministry's most difficult moment: when He would complete His purpose in becoming incarnate by dying on the cross and bringing salvation to rebellious humankind, dead by their own sins. Remember that God had already said that for there to be forgiveness of sins there must be death and shedding of blood (Leviticus 17:11; Hebrews 9:22). But notice some peculiar aspects about this scene. Read the passage again. What is the emotional state of Jesus? What request does He make of His Father? What does He conclude? What does God do for the benefit of His Son? Despite how emotional Jesus is, He does not forget who has the last word and who obeys. The redemptive plan had to be carried out, and for this the spotless Lamb, the perfect One, Jesus Christ the promised Messiah, had to die (1 Peter 1:19-21).

Finish reading Luke chapter 22 and read all of chapter 23. Jesus had a horrible public death where He experienced loss of blood, asphyxiation, exhaustion, mockery, and humiliation. His body was taken to a tomb that belonged to Joseph of Arimathea, a member of the Jewish council. It appeared that death had won. How is it possible that the Son of God died in this way, and was buried in a tomb? Thank God that's not the end. On Sunday morning, a group of women went to the grave to put spices on Jesus' body as part of the burial ritual. But what a surprise! There was no body! Jesus was not there! Read Matthew 24:1-12. Read it with a grateful heart because Jesus Christ our Savior defeated death. Sin no longer has dominion over us.

With His resurrection and the different times He appeared to various people, Jesus demonstrated that He is truly the Messiah, the Son of God. He affirmed that there is indeed salvation for the sinner. God kept His promise!

Introductory questions (10 minutes)

After a brief introduction in which you explain in your own words what you have just read, have the students participate by asking some general questions.

1. What is the most sacrificial thing a friend has ever done for you?
2. How far would you be willing to go to show a friend your love for him or her?

Development (30 minutes)

Prepare the place where you will meet and prepare the elements to take the Lord's Supper together.

To begin, tell everyone to take a quiet, personal time to pray, asking God to help them to listen and marvel at His immense love and His perfect plan to rescue and save them from sin.

Read together Luke 22:14-20 and 1 Corinthians 11:23-26.

• Who do we remember when we eat the bread and drink from the cup?
• What do these elements represent?
• What are we announcing when we drink the wine and eat the bread? Why does this remind us of the death of Jesus? For God so loved the world that He gave His only begotten Son, that whoever believes in Him should not perish but have eternal life (John 3:16).

Conclusions (10 minutes)

Why do we continue telling this story and celebrating the Lord's Supper? Why is this important for every one of us? Because we have a mission to fulfill: to announce the Good News of salvation with joy, with hope, and with courage. Let's do this, convinced that the gospel has the power to transform lives, starting with yours and mine..

Give each participant a copy of Readings from the Gospels: Arrest, Death and Resurrection of Christ at www.e625.com/lessons.

Lesson 28 > ACTS - PART ONE

In Matthew 29:19, Jesus' disciples—His followers and supporters—were entrusted with a mission. It is the same mission God always had: to redeem humanity, every person across every nation, through all of time.

God's global project is not over. Jesus the Messiah came into this world and did the will of His Father, died on a cross, and was resurrected. Now it's our turn to take the next step by announcing the good news of salvation through Jesus Christ (Acts 1:1-8).

Jesus equipped this group of disciples to fulfill the great commission. He also provided them with the basic geographical outline so that the gospel could be expanded and reach the ends of the earth.

Read Acts 1:4-5. Jesus made it clear to His disciples that they should not begin their mission until they first received "the promise." We serve a perfect God, faithful to His word and His plans. He involves people—real, imperfect human beings—in His glorious purposes. But He does not leave us alone with only our own abilities. That would make Him a cruel God, since it is impossible to fulfill the mission without the supernatural help provided by the Holy Spirit. In the 28 chapters of Acts, Luke mentions the Holy Spirit more than 50 times. The power and presence of the Holy Spirit are essential to bringing the good news and fulfilling God's plans.

The baptism of the Holy Spirit occurs only once in the life of those who believe in Christ as the Son of God, their only and sufficient Savior. This does not happen through human effort or desire, but it occurs at the moment of salvation, when the Holy Spirit takes permanent residence in the life of the believer (Romans 8:9). It occurs by the grace of God. The presence of the Holy Spirit is a promise for everyone, and it is not exclusive (Acts 2:1-4, 38-30).

Introductory questions (10 minutes)

After a brief introduction in which you explain in your own words what you have just read, have the students participate by asking some general questions.

• What are the most common obstacles you as a Christian face on a daily basis?
• What obstacles do you personally face in sharing your faith?
• Why do you think we often allow ourselves to be intimidated by these obstacles?

Development (30 minutes)

- What happened to the first followers of Jesus after His death and resurrection? Have the students read Acts 2:1-4 and 43-47.
- A promise had been made. What was it? Acts 1:4-5.
- Who can be baptized with the Holy Spirit? Acts 2:38-39.

Take some time to explain the meaning of baptism by water and baptism with the Holy Spirit. This is an excellent opportunity to review what the Bible teaches, and also to point out what your church or denomination believes on the matter.

Divide participants into groups with no more than four members in each one and ask them to brainstorm what they have heard about"what it means to be a Christian." Give them 10 minutes to think and to write down their ideas (real, radical, creative, positive, negative, etc.). Then ask at least two groups to present their ideas and have the other groups respond to what they are saying.

How do they feel about these descriptions?

We may have the wrong idea about what being a Christian is all about, and fail to live according to God's glorious purposes. Read Acts 1:8.

- We have a mission to fulfill. What is it?
- Why is it possible to fulfill it?
- For what purpose were we baptized with the Holy Spirit? To achieve our dreams and our plans, or God's plans and dreams?
- Where do we have to be witnesses? Here, there, now.

Ask them to make a list of what is their here and now, and where is their there. We are responsible for fulfilling the mission to the ends of the earth, even if we do not have time, the money, or the desire to live in another country. So how do we do this? In which active ways can we become engaged now? What plans—in the medium term and long term—can we begin to prepare for now?

- What intentional adjustments must you make to be able to live in God's plans?

Without a doubt, you are surrounded by people, friends or relatives, who do not yet believe that Jesus is the only Savior, the only way to heaven and the eternal presence of God. Ask a volunteer to read Acts 4:1-13.

- What characteristics did Paul and John have?
- In truth, how different were they from you and me?

- What was happening to them?

Now read Acts 4:23-31.

- Did they have obstacles and internal struggles?
- What was the solution? To whom did they turn to overcome their obstacles?
- What was the result?
- What are you doing about your own obstacles and struggles?

Remember: Many of those around you do not yet trust in Jesus Christ for their salvation. They have many questions, and you may have the answers. Can they tell that you know Jesus? Would they come up to you and ask you about Christ? Will you go closer to them?

Conclusions (10 minutes)

Living out God's purpose for our lives is worth it.

If we are saved, we have the Holy Spirit empowering us to be witnesses.

Take time to pray with gratitude for the Holy Spirit and the power that the Spirit gives us to fulfill our mission. Pray for courage to hold spiritual conversations in the days ahead. Pray for the people with whom you might have those conversations.

Perhaps the group can put together a "Most Wanted" list. This list will include the names of the people with whom you will seek to engage in conversation about the gospel. It is a list to pray for, and to keep track of.

Give each participant a copy of Readings from Acts, Part One, at www.e625.com/lessons.

Lesson 29 > ACTS - PART TWO

The community of Christians—the church—was growing fast. The disciples were fulfilling God's plan to bring the good news of salvation to all parts of the world through the power of the Holy Spirit. But they were already facing difficulties. Read Acts 6:8-7:1-60. If you continue reading Acts 8:1-3, you will see that the situation was only getting more complicated.

Do you remember God's plan? Where did they need to take the good news? Where were they supposed to make disciples? Review Matthew 28:19 and Acts 1:8.

Now read Acts 8:4-8. What stands out to you in these verses? The gospel had already reached Samaria. Starting with this chapter, cross-cultural encounters began to take place. This happened because even though Christ's followers were facing difficulties such as death, persecution, jail, and separation, they did not give up. They understand that they lived to fulfill a mission, and to do so, they were filled with divine Power.

Then something totally unexpected happened—but isn't that how God usually works? His plans are amazing! Read Acts 9:1-22. What is surprising? Now how far was the gospel being taken due to Saul's conversion and calling?

Just as Herod the Great tried to kill Jesus when He was a baby, so his grandson Herod in Acts 12 was trying to destroy the church. The apostles became the target. But God prepared everything so that His plan could be carried out.

Introductory questions (10 minutes)

After a brief introduction in which you explain in your own words what you have just read, have the students participate by asking some general questions.es.

* What do most people do when they face difficulties in completing a task? Why?

Development (30 minutes)

Form five teams, and assign each team one of the following passages:

1. Philip, the Samaritans, and the Ethiopian: Acts 8:4-8, 26-40
2. The great conversion: Acts 9:1-31
3. Peter and Cornelius: Acts 10

4. Peter's report: Acts 11:1-18
5. Acts 12:1-19

Remind the teams about God's plan, leading them to Matthew 28:19 and Acts 1:8. He never said that carrying out His plan was going to be easy. However, He promised to always be with His children and to give them the divine power to carry it out.

Ask each team to read the assigned passage and discuss the following questions:

1. How is God's mission evident in these passages?
2. What obstacles did the believers face?
3. What would you have done in their place?
4. What was the work of the Holy Spirit during these events?
5. What similar scenarios are we experiencing today? How are we going to face them?
6. What lessons from these verses can we put into practice today?

The gospel kept advancing and reaching other cities despite of—or thanks to—the persecution. How do you think we would react if we experienced similar persecution in our city today?

Conclusions (10 minutes)

- • God always fulfills His plans, and He does so in surprising ways.
- • If we are willing, God will ensure that the gospel advances, and use us to do so.
- • We must not look at the obstacles but at God and His plan, trusting that He will ensure that His purposes are achieved.

Take a moment to pray for the persecuted church around the world. Use the video on YouTube titled "Open Doors' World Watch List 2024."

Give each participant a copy of Readings from Acts, Part 2 at www.e625.com/lessons.

Lesson 30 > ACTS - PART THREE

We've come to the third section of Acts. Here we find the expansion of the gospel to more distant places, advancing towards the ends of the earth. Some call this section "the period of triumph."

In the midst of these chapters a new mission center emerges: Antioch of Syria, which goes from being a missionary destiny to being a source of missionaries.

Introductory questions (10 minutes)

After a brief introduction in which you explain in your own words what you have just read, have the students participate by asking some general questions.

- Who explained the gospel to you? Do you know who explained the gospel to that person? (Try to see how far you can go with your "spiritual genealogy.")
- What methods do you think are effective today in explaining the gospel to others? Which ones do you think are no longer effective?

Development (30 minutes)

As we look at the missionary journeys in this section of Acts, we find extraordinary struggles, divine interventions, adversities, conflict, joy, and obedience. We read about some new cities to which the gospel had just arrived (and later in the New Testament we will find letters full of the discipleship they received). Some new characters are introduced who will play leading roles in the development of the church. Simply put, this is an action-packed section!

So, what better than to join in?

Interview

Is your church involved in cross-cultural projects? If so, a live interview with one of those involved can be very enriching. In this interview, talk about:

1. What prompted you to go to that part of the world to work in ministry?
2. How difficult was it to make the decision to pursue this?
3. Do you think everyone should make decisions like the one you did?
4. What struggles are you currently facing in fulfilling your mission?
5. In what ways do you see the power of the Holy Spirit today?

6. What would you tell our group to get actively involved in the mission now?
7. How can we pray for you?

Going one step further, if you see fit, you can collect a special offering to support this ministry.

Investigation

One resource that can inspire and support the call to cross-cultural ministry is mission agencies. These organizations are great supports for those who undertake projects outside the country's borders. They are specialists in sending people to other regions of the world, and are communication channels that provide comprehensive support to those involved. They also serve as a link between ministry work in remote places and the local church.

Perhaps your church is already working with some missionary agencies, or your denomination itself has such an organization. Look for these organizations in your country and establish contact with them so they can visit your group and present the work they do. If they can't meet in person, you could arrange a phone interview.

The objective is to inform the members of your group about what these agencies do, engaging them and awakening their interest. A smaller amount of clear and concise information will be much more impactful than trying to cover every possible topic, which will only bore your audience and lose their interest.

You may be able to get representatives from some agencies to come to your meeting and tell stories, providing take-home materials to your group. Don't be discouraged if no one immediately decides to pursue a missionary calling to another country. That's not the goal. The important thing is that they learn about these opportunities. The Lord may inspire some of them later in life with projects like these. Because of interviews like this one they will already know where they can find support in what they are called to pursue.

Action

Traveling to distant places with different cultures requires great effort. Keep these in your sight and include them in your future plans, but start now with small steps. Invite your group to plan a cross-cultural visit within your city. Maybe you know someone at an organization that works with children at risk, or at a nursing home. Orphanages, hospitals, street ministries, and schools in rural or urban areas can also be places where your group can build relationships as they step out of their comfort zone.

These projects can last anywhere from a couple of hours to a full day. Over time you could go further, to other cities or towns, or to other countries. Step by step the challenge becomes greater. Step by step the faith it requires is greater.

So, give the group the challenge of organizing a project to implement within the next few days. It may help if you already have the place and time in mind. Ask the group to define what things they can do on this visit to bring hope with the gospel, and how they can thoughtfully and compassionately learn from those they meet. Think about ways you can create a program that facilitates spiritual discussions and meet real needs. The program can include songs, crafts, testimonies, dramas, games, preparing a meal, delivering clothing or medicine, some service or physical work, and much more in addition to conversations about spiritual topics. Remind students these conversations don't require memorizing dialogue, answering every concern, or bombarding anyone with biblical passages. When you spend time with people, it is always a chance for mutual learning about spiritual and other topics.

Delegate the logistics of planning to members of the group, helping them to make plans for finances and other important elements.

We cannot solve all the problems of those we visit in one afternoon. In fact, we might learn as much about ourselves as they learn from us. Those we meet might influence our own faith and inspire us. These experiences leave indelible marks. Shared conversations, shared meals, and helping others meet their needs can bring us hope and encouragement. Without a doubt, the biggest mark will be the one that remains in our hearts.

Conclusiones (10')

The mission is not a suggestion but a commandment. The church of Christ must reach to the ends of the earth, and all Christians share that responsibility. The book of Acts continues through us. Close today's class by praying for the world in need of Christ and for the compassion, obedience, and courage your group needs to advance the mission.

Give each participant a copy of Readings from Acts, Part 3 at www.e625.com/lessons.

Lesson 31 > ACTS - PART FOUR

The last part of the book of Acts has a main protagonist, Saul (or Paul). Saul had an encounter with God and the course of his life was changed forever. He went from persecuting, imprisoning, and killing Christians to being one of the most influential followers of Jesus.

Just as God had told Ananias (Acts 9:15-16), Saul would preach the message of salvation to both kings and commoners. Saul was passionate about God, and he embarked on a lifelong journey to fulfill the mission for which he had been called.

Introductory questions (10 minutes)

After a brief introduction in which you explain in your own words what you have just read, have the students participate by asking some general questions.

1. What is the longest trip that you have ever taken?
2. What trip would you like to take? How long would it be? How many stops would you make and why would you choose those places?
3. Who would you take with you on those trips if you could, and why?

This last section of the book of Acts is marked by the missionary journeys and the cities visited during those journeys. Saul's conversion was a key event. It was unexpected due to Saul's hatred and persecution of Christians, and decisive due to the subsequent growth and extension of the church that resulted. When you go through these pages you will witness the beginning of something that has never stopped, something that has to do with the last commandment of Jesus: taking the gospel to every corner of the earth.

Development (30 minutes)

This is the outline of this part of the book of Acts:

Chapters 13-28: The testimony to the ends of the earth.

1 - The spread of the church in Asia Minor and Europe: 13:1-21:17
- Paul's first missionary journey: 13:1-14:28
- The Jerusalem Council: 15:1-35
- Paul's second missionary journey: 15:36-18:22
- Paul's third missionary journey: 18:23-21:17

2 - The extension of the church in Rome: 21:18-28:31
- Paul's trials: 21:18-26:32
- Paul preaches the gospel in Rome: 27:1-28:31

Group reading:

Read Acts 13:1-5 aloud for everyone. Tell the group that this passage marks a beginning nobody could have imagined at the time. Paul would become one of the most important missionaries in history. Many cities and people would find God through Paul's unique story, which continues to influence us today.

Exercise:

Divide your young people into small groups of 5 to 7 people each. Assign each group a small group leader or a group member who will be in charge of asking the questions below. Take approximately 10 minutes for each of the three points. Set the stage to make students feel comfortable answering the questions and sharing honestly.

1 - God can impact hard hearts
- Do you have friends or acquaintances who are firmly opposed to the faith, people you have trouble imagining as Christians?
Describe them.
- In your opinion, what would be the best strategy to share the gospel with them?
- If they were to have an important encounter with God, do you think they would later become influential in spreading the message of the cross?

2 - God calls people to serve Him
- Does God have only one way of calling people? Try to remember different ways God called people in the Bible.
- Do you know people who have a clear understanding of God's calling for them? What stands out to you about them and that calling?
- Do you have a clear sense of God's purpose for your life? If you do, what can you share about it?

3 - God does not look for superheroes
- When you think about God calling someone for a special mission, what characteristics do you imagine that person should have?
- Do you believe that God can use you just as you are?
- Are there people who will not be willing to accept the mission God entrusts to them? What should someone with faith do if they begin a conversation or relationship with someone like that?

Conclusions (10 minutes)

After the group exercise, take the lead again from the front and, using your own words, prepare a micro message that affirms the topics discussed. Here's some help:

Saul was one of those people who seemed extremely unlikely to convert to Christianity. He was full of hatred and threats, but God met him and transformed him. The Lord got Paul to channel all of his personality, knowledge, passion, and firmness to become a true titan of the gospel, one who preached to thousands of people and planted dozens of churches.

God can soften anyone's heart, even those of our friends we have a hard time imagining as followers of Jesus. We must share the message with those around us regardless, because God wants to have a relationship with each of us, and only God knows how He will use and impact us.

Paul and his contemporaries were the first Christian missionaries. Throughout history, many people have brought the Word of Salvation to others, and thousands of them have suffered, and some have died in unknown lands, far from their families, for the sake of the gospel. Like Jesus, they gave their lives to bring salvation to those who otherwise would never have known Him, as could have been our case. The Lord continues to call His children to join the great enterprise Jesus entrusted to us: reaching all corners of the world with His Word, with His love, and with His salvation. Do we see ourselves as part of this mission? Are we doing all we can to shine the light of Christ? How will we respond to God's calling in our lives?

Close with a prayer that we will not be indifferent to the spiritual needs of those around us. You could also use a song your students like and that relates to this message.

Give each participant a copy of Readings from Acts, part 4 at www.e625.com/lessons.

Lección 32 > JAMES

The epistle of James begins as a letter and ends more like a sermon. It is like a collection of messages from a pastor who knows his congregation well. It is believed that the author was James, the half-brother of Jesus (Mark 6:3) and its content is focused on Christians practicing what they have learned, rather than focusing only on words. The letter is rich in timely themes, relevant to a person's daily walk with God.

Introductory questions (10 minutes)

After a brief introduction in which you explain in your own words what you have just read, have the students participate by asking some general questions.

1 – Do you look at yourself in the mirror often? How many times a day, would you guess?
2- Can you imagine what life would be like without mirrors? Describe it.
3- What do you think would happen if you were only allowed to look at yourself in the mirror, but you couldn't then fix your hair, your face, or your clothes?

In this letter from the Bible, we are invited to look at ourselves in the mirror, not just to notice what we see, but to act by fixing what is not right.

Development (30 minutes)

This is the outline of the book, to enable you to place yourself in the context of each topic and study it before your class.

Outline of the themes of the letter of James

1. Trials 1:2-1-8
2. Perseverance in suffering: 1:9-12
3. Temptation: 1:13-18
4. Putting the Word into practice: 1:19-27
5. Impartial love: 2:1-13
6. Righteous works: 2:14-26
7. The tongue: 3:1-12
8. Wisdom: 3:13-18
9. Desires and passions: 4:1-12
10. Dependence on humility: 4:13-17

11. Justice: 5:1:6
12. Patience with faith: 5:7-11
13. Truthfulness: 5:12
14. Prayer: 5:13-18
15. Bringing back a lost person: 5:19-20

Group exercise:

Divide your young people into small groups of 5 to 7 people. Assign a leader to each group to lead discussion using the questions below, either an adult volunteer or one of the students. Take approximately 10 minutes for each of the three points. Help set the stage for students to share openly.

1 - When our faith is tested. Read James 1:2-4.
- What difficult circumstances might test our faith?
- Are temptations tests of what we believe, and what might that look like?
- How can a gift, a blessing, or something good from God to us become a test for our faith?

2 - To learn, but not practice. Read James 1:22-25.
- In what sense is the Bible a mirror for our lives?
- What practical and concrete steps can we take to avoid becoming simple hearers of the Word of God?
- What negative effects does a simple hearer of the Word spread, and what positive effects does a doer of the Word spread?

3 - Faith and works. Read James 2:14-19.
- • Can you do good works without having faith? Do you know good people who don't know God?
- • Can you have faith without works? Do you know people who know a lot but make questionable choices in how they live?
- • What is the best way to demonstrate our faith and prove that it is genuine?

Conclusions (10 minutes)

One of the main reasons people do not want to get involved in the church today is the great gap they see between what many Christians say they believe and how they actually live. Regardless of each person's intentions, this is usually summarized in one word: hypocrisy.

Nobody wants to be a hypocrite, but if we do not pay special attention to our actions and attitudes, we will become exactly what we condemn in other persons. People pick up on our beliefs, what we support, and how we teach. When those things don't reflect the love and teachings of God, others see our hypocrisy.

At a time when society has almost no tolerance for falsehood and doublespeak, we Christians are exhorted by James to live what we believe and put into practice what we hear.

The Bible serves as a mirror that shows us the true state of our hearts. What will we do about it? Will we let it change us?

Finish by reading James 2:26. "For as the body apart from the spirit is dead, so also faith apart from works is dead."

Give each participant a copy of Readings from James at www.e625.com/lessons.

Lesson 33 > GALATIANS

The letter to the Galatians was written by Paul to the churches in Galatia that had Jewish and non-Jewish (Gentile) members. At first, the Galatians had understood the grace of God and the origin of salvation, but now many teachers wanted to impose Jewish law, including circumcision, on non-Jews as a requirement for becoming Christians.

In response, Paul wrote to the Galatians to defend justification by faith. The central theme of the book is freedom in Christ against the legalism of tradition and law.

Introductory questions (10 minutes)

After a brief introduction in which you explain in your own words what you have just read, have the students participate by asking some general questions.

1. What are some examples of things that start well but end badly?
2. Will anyone share an anecdote about when this has happened to you?
3. What is something you are involved in that you want to end well? What precautions can you take to avoid becoming careless and having it end up very different from how it began?

The Galatians had started well in their walk with God, but after some time, pressured by bad influences, they lost focus on Christianity and became prisoners of practices and traditions that had nothing to do with what God asked of them.

Development (30 minutes)

We can categorize the book of Galatians as follows:

1. Personal - The apostle and justification by faith: 1:1-2:21.
2. Doctrinal - The principles of justification by faith: 3:1-4:31.
3. Practical - The privileges of justification by faith: 5:1-6:18.

Group exercise:

Divide your young people into small groups of 5 to 7 people each. Assign each group a student or leader to lead the discussion using the questions below. Take approximately 10 minutes for each of the three points, and do everything in your power to get the young people to speak and express their opinions.

1 - Slavery vs. Freedom

- What images come to mind when you think about slavery?
- Name the first thing that goes through your head when the word

"freedom" is mentioned.
- What are current examples of slavery and freedom that can be applied to the way we live our Christianity today?

2 - Legalism and traditions
- How can we distinguish a divine commandment or principle from a simple tradition?
- Why do you think many Christians fall prey to customs and traditions that have no biblical basis?
- Can we use the freedom that God gave us so poorly that we end up distancing ourselves from Him? Give some examples.

3 - Feeding the Spirit to our sinful nature.
Read Galatians 5:19-26
- How would you explain in your own words that obeying God brings you freedom and disobeying Him enslaves you?
- In which things and in which ways can we feed our old nature so that it dominates us?
- In what concrete way can we feed the Holy Spirit within us, to keep us from enslaving ourselves with traditions we don't need to keep and help us to enjoy the freedom that God brings?

Conclusions (10 minutes)

Think about those things that are enslaving you and preventing you from enjoying freedom in Christ. They may be practices, traditions (as in the case of the Galatians), an obsession with pleasing other people, or a poorly learned Christianity that is limited to religiously complying with rules and restrictions.

It may also be that you are feeding your sinful old nature, which we all naturally do unless we voluntarily and intentionally allow ourselves to be guided by the Holy Spirit and nurtured by the life of God in us. The devil and the world are experts at disguising as good what is evil, and slowly blinding us to sins that harm us and distance us from God's beautiful plan for us.

Sometimes we end up becoming slaves to our own wrong way of thinking, for example, by focusing on our insecurities, exaggerated focus on ourselves, a high dose of pride and selfishness, and poor self-esteem from our unhealthy comparisons with others.

God came into our lives to bring us freedom from anything that seeks to bind us. He is our Lord and we do not need any other master to take over our decisions and will.

The divine purpose for our lives is the best thing that can happen to us, enabling us to enjoy lives of freedom and fulfillment. Let's work on that, and not in satisfying our natural desires.

Give each participant a copy of Readings from Galatians, downloadable at www.e625.com/lessons.

Lesson 34 > 1 AND 2 THESSALONIANS

Paul is the author of the two letters to the church in Thessalonica, and with him were his collaborators and traveling companions Silas and Timothy. It is believed that he wrote these letters while they were in Corinth between 51 and 52 AD. In these epistles Paul addresses the topic of hope in Christ, His second coming, and its effects. Studying both letters, we also find exhortations that remain relevant today to keep our hope firm and to live properly and maturely. We will focus on some of these exhortations in this lesson.

Introductory questions (10 minutes)

After a brief introduction in which you explain in your own words what you have just read, have the students participate by asking some general questions.

Have you ever been owed money and spent it on something before you'd actually be paid? What would have been more advisable in that situation?

If someone told you that you would soon get a better job, but they didn't specify when, would you leave your current job to just wait for the new one?

Some Thessalonians, poorly influenced by false revelations, were so enthusiastically embracing the hope of the second coming of Jesus to earth that they had begun to abandon their responsibilities and leave their jobs to dedicate themselves to waiting for the Lord. Paul exhorted them in the second letter by explaining that the Lord had not yet come, writing, "Whoever does not want to work should not eat either…"

Development (30 minutes)

The outline of these epistles could be the following:

1 Thessalonians:
1. Paul's greeting: 1:1
2. Personal reflections: 1:2-3:13
3. Paul's practical instructions: 4:1-5:22
4. Final blessing: 5:23-24
5. Closing comments: 5:25-28

2 Thessalonians:
1. Paul's greeting: 1:1-2
2. Paul's comfort in persecution: 1:3-12
3. Warning and exhortation to perseverance: 2:1-17

4. Teachings in action: 3:1-15
5. Final greetings: 3:16-18

Group exercise:
Divide your group into small groups of 5 to 7 people each. Assign each group a leader or student to ask the questions below. Take approximately 10 minutes for each of the three points, and encourage your students to speak openly and share their thoughts.

1) The second coming of the Lord.
Read 1 Thessalonians 4:13-5:3
- What feelings does the idea of the second coming of Christ to earth generate in you?
- What did Paul mean when he stated that Jesus will come like a thief in the night?
- We cannot dedicate ourselves only to waiting for the second coming of Jesus. Instead, we must focus on making good use of our time. What might that look like?

2) Joyful and grateful.
Read 1 Thessalonians 5:16-18
- Why don't most people live joyfully and gratefully?
- Do you think it is possible to live "always joyfully" and give thanks "in everything"?
What did Paul mean?
- How do you think gratitude is related to joy??

3) Pray without ceasing
- Can you explain in your own words what it means to pray without ceasing?
- What, in your opinion, are the main reasons why we do not pray more?
- What specific things could we do to be able to enjoy talking and chatting with God more?

Conclusions (10 minutes)

The coming of the Lord is the most glorious hope we have as Christians. Knowing that this will happen should encourage us to do everything in our power to fulfill God's will. We should be preparing, studying, and working to be true reflections of the light of God in the society in which we live.

We should expect the second coming as if it is going to happen tonight, but at the same time we should plan and work as if the Lord is going to return many years from now.

Being grateful helps us value and enjoy everything God gives us. We must cultivate this attitude so that gratitude becomes our lifestyle. Always being happy and joyful has much more to do with who we are than with what we have.

Both gratitude and complaining are highly contagious. Let us keep this in mind when choosing our relationships and when we think of the words we share with others.

Close with a time of prayer in groups of two.

Give each participant a copy of Readings from 1 and 2 Thessalonians at www.e625.com/lessons.

Lesson 35 > 1 CORINTHIANS

As the first verse of this letter says, the author is Paul. He probably wrote it midway through 55 AD, from the city of Ephesus, during his third missionary journey. Paul was hoping to visit the Corinthians soon. The letter to the church in Corinth focuses on helping believers to become mature in Christ, correcting some false teachings that were intruding in the church, and reminding them of the sacrifice on the cross and especially of the resurrection of Jesus for the sanctification of believers in Christ.

Introductory questions (10 minutes)

After a brief introduction in which you explain in your own words what you have just read, have the students participate by asking some general questions.

1. What is a church?
2. What kind of people make up a church?
3. Is the church perfect? Why not? What would a perfect church be like?

In the church of Corinth there were several leaders. Perhaps today we would call them pastors or elders. The people of the church were comparing them against each other. Paul reminded them of the essence of the church and used the letter to also touch on other topics, some of which we will focus on in this lesson.

Development (30 minutes)

We can outline the letter to the Corinthians as follows:
1. Introduction: 1:1-9
2. Division in the church: 1:10-4:21
3. Disorder in the church: 5:1-6:20
4. Difficulties in the church: 7:1-14:40
5. The hope of the church, the resurrection: 15:1-58
6. A charge to the church, practical and personal matters: 16:1-24

Group exercise

Divide your group into small groups of 5 to 7 people. Assign each group a student or leader who will lead a discussion on the questions below. Take approximately 10 minutes for each of the three points, encouraging students to share openly and honestly about each topic.

1 - Sexuality. Read 1 Corinthians 6:18-20.
- How is the concept God provides about sex so different from what current society promotes?
- How does the sin of sexual immorality compare to other types of sin?
- What implications does the fact that our body is a temple of the Holy Spirit have on our sexuality and other issues related to our physical appearance?

2 - Many members, one body. Read 1 Corinthians 12:14-26.
- What similarities do you find between the members of the human body and the members of a church? Why would God want Paul to use this example?
- What are reasons some Christians do not feel unity with the rest of the body that is the church?
- What should be our view and our attitude toward those brothers and sisters in faith who do not think the same way we do?

3 - True love. Read 1 Corinthians 13.
- What characteristics of the love described in this chapter are the most difficult to find or enact today?
- Doesn't it seem like God is asking for a lot when He tells us to have this kind of love? Why?
- List some reasons why many Christians find it difficult to practice this true love in their relationships as couples and families.

Conclusions (10 minutes)

In the church, we need everyone. As in a body, not all members can do the same things, because we have different abilities, talents, and gifts from God. The important thing is for us to never forget that we are each part of a whole, and that the head of that whole is Christ.

We need leaders, pastors, and teachers, but we also need all the other members to accomplish all the other things that the church must do. We must live in harmony and subject ourselves to the true government of the church, which is divine. Divisions, comparisons, contempt, and envy only indicate spiritual immaturity. Let's never get involved in such things.

What Paul mentions as the most excellent way is a great antidote to the divisions we've talked about: Love. True love that is not selfish, that is not proud or resentful, and that rejoices in the truth should be the bond that unites us in the church and in the service of our Lord. Otherwise, what we do for God will be in vain.

This kind of love is what we have to give to all our loved ones. Spouses, children,

family, and friends. A child of God who reflects well his Heavenly Father loves with this kind of love, which is very different from the world's versions of "love" that we see today.
Our bodies are temples of the Holy Spirit. That is why our sexuality is not a minor issue for God.

Taking care of our body is not only related to a sexual life obedient to God, but in all things related to our health and well-being. Being responsible and loving toward our bodies also honors God.

Close by praying for your young people to remain pure for God and for each of them to occupy the place God intended for them within the body that is the church. And pray also that they can be faithful practitioners of the version of love proclaimed by Him who is love.

Give each participant a copy of Readings from 1 Corinthians, downloadable at www.e625.com/lessons.

Lesson 36 › 2 CORINTHIANS

Paul writes this second letter to the Corinthians approximately a year after the first. False prophets had interfered in the church of Corinth and had raised up the brethren against Paul, so the apostle immediately went to visit them. His visit did not go well: Paul was not treated as he deserved. Paul returned to Ephesus and from there he wrote to the Corinthians with clarity and, where needed, necessary harshness.

This is an intensely personal letter, written in the context of conflict with those who attacked Paul's mission and authority. However, even that tense situation did not stop Paul from sharing some heart-felt teachings.

Introductory questions (10 minutes)

After a brief introduction in which you explain in your own words what you have just read, have the students participate by asking some general questions.

1. Of the inspiring messages that usually appear on social media, do any of them stand out in your memory? What made them memorable?
2. Have you ever come up with an inspirational message of your own? Can you share it with us?
3. Have you ever had a memorable quote or mantra genuinely help you during a difficult time?

Note: *If your group does not come up with answers, you can look online for inspirational phrases to use as examples, and modify the questions to be about them.*

Paul had visited Corinth but left the city sad because of some confrontations he had there. His first letter to the church at Corinth had been somewhat harsh. On a return journey to Rome he could have stopped in Corinth but decided not to because he was still somewhat hurt and did not want to act on impulse.

He then wrote the Corinthians a letter full of feeling and love, enough to make endless memes and inspirational quotes. You'll see when we read it together.

Development (30 minutes)

The second letter to the Corinthians can be outlined as follows:

1. Introduction: 1:1-11

2. Paul's ministry: 1:12-7:16
3. Collection: 8:1-9:15
4. Credentials: 10:1-12:13
5. The visit: 12:14-13:10
6. Blessing: 13:11-14

Group exercise

Divide your young people into small groups of 5 to 7 people each. Assign a volunteer or student to lead the discussion in each group using the questions below. Take approximately 10 minutes for each of the three points. Encourage your group to share openly.

1 - Resolving conflicts. Read 2 Corinthians 2:5-11.
- Have you ever been at odds with someone, so much so that it caused a separation that lasted a long time? How did you finally resolve the issue (if you did)?
- Describe a high-conflict person, someone who has problems with others wherever they go.
- According to Paul's example in this letter, how should Christians approach conflicts?

2 – Peacemakers.
- Name some concrete ways of establishing peace at a time when wars, fights, and splits are everywhere in daily life.
- How can we be instruments to share the peace of God with others, both those who know Him and those who do not?
- How might God use us to be peacemakers within the church?

3 - Reconciliation. Read 2 Corinthians 5:18-20.
- What has to happen for two estranged parties to reconcile?
- What are the most difficult things about asking for forgiveness, and about forgiving someone else?
- In this passage Paul says Christ-followers are ambassadors in charge of the ministry of reconciliation. How would you describe that role?

Conclusions (10 minutes)

After the group time, take the lead from the front and prepare in your own words a short message that affirms the topics already discussed. Here are some tips:

Paul wrote to the Corinthian church after they'd had some difficult interactions. He told them with love how he felt, and how knowledge in the Lord united and restored them. He reminded them of the things that are important and the things that are not.

His last visit to Corinth had not gone very well with some members of the church there. But Paul did not sit quietly trying to forget, nor did he put himself in the role of someone who is offended and puts all of the responsibility on the other party to make things right.

God's love was reflected in Paul's ways. Paul knew that although those who had caused problems had to be rebuked, it was also important to restore them and love them again, showing God's love so that they could learn to walk in the truth.

We must not remain passive about disagreements that have distanced us from others. It is God's will that as far as it depends on us, we are at peace with the whole world. Let's ask ourselves: Where do we have unresolved conflicts with others? As we work toward reconciliation, not only are we restoring our relationships, but we are fulfilling our role as ambassadors, helping more and more people to be reconciled with God.

Give each participant a copy of Readings from 2 Corinthians, downloadable at www.e625.com/lessons.

Lesson 37 > ROMANS

The name of this epistle comes from its recipients: the believers in the church in Rome, the capital of the Roman Empire. Paul, the author of this letter, was a Roman citizen from the city of Tarsus.

Paul was responsible for the spread of the gospel throughout the Roman Empire. After returning from Jerusalem to Rome he had been falsely accused, beaten, and taken into Roman custody. After a short time of freedom in which he was able to travel, he was once again arrested. He died a martyr in Rome around 66-67 AD.

Paul wrote to the church in Rome from Corinth in around 56 AD. This book of the Bible is above all a doctrinal letter. It declares that what justifies the human sinner before God is faith in Jesus on the cross, which sanctifies us and reconciles us with the eternal Father.

Introductory questions (10 minutes)

After a brief introduction in which you explain in your own words what you have just read, have the students participate by asking some general questions.

1. Have you ever (even as a child) done something wrong and been caught? What did you do and how did you get caught?
2. Have you ever justified your actions by saying, "Everyone does it"?
3. Have you ever been punished when others were not, even though you had all gotten into mischief together? How did it happen?

We've all been caught in not-so-honorable moments and suffered the consequences. You have most likely taken the blame at some point for something that other people were also involved in. Or maybe you are the one who was able to get away with things while others got caught.

It is very unusual for someone who didn't do anything wrong to want to take the blame. Who would do that? Shouldn't the person who did wrong be the one to deal with the consequences? Paul tells a story of a counterintuitive situation. In this letter to the church in Rome, he reminds his readers of a story of sacrifice, undeserved punishment, and love.

Development (30 minutes)

The outline of the epistle to the Romans could be the following:

1. Introduction: 1:1-17
2. Damnation - sinful humanity: 1:18-3:20
3. Justification - the justice of God: 3:21-5:21
4. Sanctification - glorified and set apart for God: 6:1-8:39
5. Restoration - God's plan: 9:1-11:36
6. Attitude - the conduct of God's justice: 12:1-15:13
7. Recommendations, greetings, and final blessing: 15:14-16:27

Group exercise

Divide your young people into small groups of 5 to 7 people each. Assign a student or leader to guide the discussion for each group based on the prompts below. Take approximately 10 minutes for each of the three points. Encourage students to have an open, honest discussion.

1 - The truth about sin.

- Have you ever wondered what you would have done if you faced the temptations Adam and Eve did in Eden?
- In your opinion, do people today find it difficult to accept and recognize that they are sinners?
- How would you explain the verse (6:23) that says "the wages of sin is death"?

2 - Saved by faith and not by works. Read Romans 3:21-26

- What would our lives be like if salvation could be achieved through our own effort (or works)?
- Do you think that the people in heaven have done many works? Haven't done many works? Some of both? Why?
- James wrote that faith without works is dead. What is your opinion of that statement?

3 - Justification. Read Romans 5:1-2

- Has someone ever paid for something on your behalf? Can you comment on how you felt?
- How would you explain to a friend in simple words that thanks to Jesus' sacrifice on the cross we are now justified forever with God?
- What is the difference between living to please a God who has already paid your debt, versus always trying to fulfill your debt by accumulating merits to look better in God's eyes?

Conclusions (10 minutes)

The story of the cross happened almost 2,000 years ago, but it impacts all human beings. When Jesus sacrificed Himself, He was thinking about you and me. He saw our faces and knew our names. His love for us is why He didn't get off the cross. Jesus knew that His sacrifice would save the lives of His friends and of all human beings for as long as humans exist.

This kind of sacrifice escapes all human logic, but God's unconditional love has no limits. Jesus came to live on earth, fully God and fully human, and paid a debt we could never have. If we place our faith in Jesus and His sacrifice, God sees us as righteous.

Our good works can never save us; it is faith that justifies us before God. As James writes, faith without works is dead.

Just as the first step to our salvation was to recognize our sin, we must be God's instruments, sharing love with others so that they can experience God's sacrificial mercy, too. God continues to demonstrate His love for us even when are sinners (Romans 5:8)

Close with a prayer of repentance, surrender, and gratitude for Jesus Christ's sacrifice on the cross. Give thanks for this wonderful story that has changed our lives and that can also change the lives of anyone who so desires.

Give each participant a copy of Readings from Romans, downloadable at www.e625.com/lessons.

Lesson 38 > EPHESIANS

Ephesians is one of the group of letters that Paul wrote while he was held captive in Rome, alongside Philippians, Colossians, and Philemon. These letters are known as the "prison epistles," or "captivity epistles." The letter to the church in Ephesus was written between 60-62 AD. This letter, along with the letter to the Colossians, emphasizes that the church is the body of Christ and Christ is the head. Among other topics, it talks about gifts, offers instructions for the family, and details about how to prepare ourselves to fight our battles as Christians.

Introductory questions (10 minutes)

After a brief introduction in which you explain in your own words what you have just read, have the students participate by asking some general questions.

1. What kinds of sentiments or good wishes do people typically write, like on a birthday card?
2. Why do we extend good wishes to others? On which occasions do we do this?
3. To whom do we generally extend good wishes? Why don't we offer good wishes to strangers?

In his letter to the church in Ephesus, Paul reminds them of essential teachings and gives them new advice. He seems so happy with his friends in this city that he begins by offering them many good wishes, and then encourages them to act in unity and be strengthened in God's truths.

Development (30 minutes)

Paul's letter to the believers in Ephesus can be outlined as follows:
1. Greetings: 1:1-2
2. The believer in Christ: 1:3-3:13
   - Predestination: 1:3-6
   - Redemption: 1:6-10
   - Inheritance: 1:11-14
   - Revelation: 1:15-23
   - New Life: 2:1-10
   - Unity: 2:11-3:13
3. God's plan for the church: 3:14-6:9
   - Fullness: 3:14-21
   - Unity: 4:1-6

- Training and edification: 4:7-16
- Life in the light: 4:17-32
- Life as examples: 5-6:9
4. God's power for the church: 6:10-20
5. Final greetings: 6:21-24

Group exercise
Divide your young people into small groups of 5 to 7 people. Assign each group a leader or student to guide the discussion based on the prompts below. Take approximately 10 minutes for each of the three points.

1 - Gifts. Read Ephesians 4:7-13.
- If the owner of the gifts and the one who distributes them is God, how should we feel about the gifts we have?
- According to the Bible, are some gifts more important than others?
- What would you say to someone who boasts about a spiritual gift he or she has?

2 - Family. Read Ephesians 5:21-33
- What differences do you notice between most marriages today and what Paul proposes in this passage?
- Based on your experience as a child, what things were most difficult about obeying and honoring your parents?
- Why do you think the family and its private relationships are so important to God?

3 - Armor. Read Ephesians 6:10-17.
- According to this classic Bible passage, who is our fight against? How would you explain this?
- What part of this armor draws your attention the most and why?
- Since our true fight is not against human beings, how should we look at people who might appear as enemies?

Conclusions (10 minutes)
God chose to distribute gifts to all His children. These gifts are not ours, so they should not be sources of pride, nor should we enter into meaningless comparisons that lead us to other sins such as looking down on or envying others.

The Lord in His wisdom and sovereignty knows why He gave particular gifts to each person. His idea is that in the church we function as a true team, using those gifts by serving one another. The gifts have no other purpose than to serve others and glorify God. Have you already discovered your gifts? Share with your students that if they start serving in whatever way they can right now, God will show them their gifts.

Whatever role we occupy within our family, this letter contains advice and commandments for us. If we are going to start a family one day, let us do so on the basis of the Word of God, first between spouses and then by spreading it to our future children. Let us establish these biblical tips as family norms and rules that will bless us all.

The Bible always tells the truth, and it doesn't say anywhere that living the Christian life will be easy. In this letter today, we were given the details of the weapons we should use to defend ourselves and to attack. What Ephesians makes very clear is that our struggles are not against human beings, but against spiritual forces of evil.

Let us not waste time seeing other people as enemies, and let us focus on the true identity of our adversary.

Each part of the armor plays a fundamental role. Let us memorize the complete armor and make correct and constant use of it.

You can close in prayer by asking that your young people be well-armed Christians and ready to fight the right fights. Also ask that they may find the place God intends for them within the church according to the gifts that they've received.

Give each participant a copy of Readings from Ephesians at www.e625.com/lessons.

Lesson 39 > PHILIPPIANS

Philippians is derived from the Greek city called Philippi, named after Philip II of Macedonia, father of Alexander the Great. The city was strategically located as a gateway to Europe. Philippi was the first place in Macedonia where Paul founded a church, and it became the cradle of Christianity in Europe. This letter is believed to have been written around 61 AD, after Paul's imprisonment in Rome. The letter to the church in Philippi is Paul's most personal and affectionate.

Introductory questions (10 minutes)

After a brief introduction in which you explain in your own words what you have just read, have the students participate by asking some general questions.

1. Have you ever lied, or done something just to impress somebody? What did you do?
2. How long do you think appearances can be kept up? Why?

In Paul's letter to the Philippians, he begins by greeting them with great affection, but he soon mentions that there are some people preaching out of envy and rivalry. Even in Paul's time, there were people doing things seemingly out of goodness but actually motivated by unfocused or even negative interests.

Development (30 minutes)

The outline of this epistle could be the following:
1. Greeting: 1:1-2
2. Thanksgiving and prayer: 1:3-11
3. Imprisoned for Christ: 1:12-26
4. Paul's exhortations: 1:27-2:18
5. Standing firm in persecution: 1:27-30
6. United in humility: 2:1-4
7. Remembering the example of Jesus: 2:5-11
8. Being a light: 2:12-18
9. Paul's companions: 2:19-30
10. Timothy: 2:19-24
11. Epaphroditus: 2:25-30
12. Paul's example: 3:1-21
13. Paul's advice : 4:1-9
14. Thanksgiving and final greeting: 4:10-23

Group exercise

Divide your young people into small groups of 5 to 7 people each. If it is not possible for each small group to have a leader who can play the role of moderator, make sure one member of each group has the following questions to serve as prompts for today's discussion. Take approximately 10 minutes for each of the three points, and do everything you can to encourage your students to share openly.

1 - Humility. Read Philippians 2:2-4
- What is your definition of humility?
- How can we become contaminated by vanity and selfishness?
- When is it hard for you to think of others as superior to yourself? In what circumstances?

2 - The same feeling. Read Philippians 2:5-11
- Name three attitudes of Jesus from this passage that we should imitate.

3 - Contentment. Read Philippians 4:10-13.
- What is the true context of the famous phrase, "I can do all things through Christ who strengthens me"?
- Some say that God's will is for us to be poor, and others say exactly the opposite. Based on these verses, what are your thoughts?
- What is something that seems key to being happy and content beyond the economic circumstances we go through?

Conclusions (10 minutes)

Humility is a virtue God produces in us if we allow Him to. Rivalry, envy, or vanity should never be our motivation to do something. The advice to consider others as superior ourselves is an excellent starting point as we aim to be excellent representatives of a God who is, paradoxically, an expert in humility.

Many things could be said about Jesus' humility, from His birth, His life, and even His last days here on earth. The graphic way in which this letter describes Christ's descent and humiliation might leave us amazed when we try to understand what it all meant to Him.

We are being asked to have the same attitude. Not to cling to what we may have achieved or to a position that gives us recognition or makes us feel fulfilled, but rather to be willing to always give up what is necessary for love.

Paul was an example of contentment. In his case, he adapted to the economic condition he had to go through. As he himself tells it, he went through moments of abundance and scarcity and neither of these situations affected his heart. He affirmed that he was prepared for everything because with Christ's strength, everything is possible.

We must be grateful for everything we have and for our present circumstances. We must not be mediocre conformists who just want to stay where they are, but we must also not have excessive ambition. We must practice contentment by enjoying and being thankful for what we have.

The best thing we can do is imitate Paul in being prepared for every situation, which likely means avoiding what some people teach about finances, even what they proclaim as God's view of finances. It is not true that God wants us all to be rich, nor is it true that He wants us all to be poor. Rather, there are different times in each person's life, there are different divine plans for different people, and there are also different personal dispositions and decisions. Going through a time of financial ease or hardship does not automatically indicate some spiritual state.

We can close by praying that our young people will be humble and that they will seek contentment and gratitude in their ways of living and acting.

Give each participant a copy of Readings from Philippians, downloadable at www.e625.com/lessons.

Lesson 40 > COLOSSIANS

Paul wrote this letter to the church that was meeting in Colossae (present-day Turkey), with the suggestion that it be shared with their neighbors in Laodicea. The church had been growing, and false doctrines and philosophies were imminent threats. Paul's central objective for this letter is that Jesus Christ is God, and His sacrifice on the cross refocuses our lives toward a new identity. Colossians is a short letter with a lot of powerful content.

Introductory questions (10 minutes)

After a brief introduction in which you explain in your own words what you have just read, have the students participate by asking some general questions..

1. Have you ever tripped because you were walking while distracted and looking elsewhere?
2. Have you ever witnessed an accident caused by someone driving while distracted?

In this letter we will see, among other things, the urgent need to keep our eyes on what matters so as not to stumble or suffer any spiritual accident we'll regret.

Development (30 minutes)

The structure of Colossians can be thought of as follows:

1. Paul's greetings and prayer: 1:1-14
2. Doctrinal instructions: 1:15-2:23
3. The deity of Christ: 1:15-23
4. Paul's ministry: 1:24-2:7
5. False doctrines: 2:8-23
6. Practical instructions: 3:1-4:18
7. Rules for living a holy life: 3:1-17
8. Rules for the family: 3:18-4:1
9. Additional instructions: 4:2-18

Group exercise

Divide your young people into small groups of 5 to 7 people each. If it is not possible for each small group to have a leader who can play the role of moderator, make sure that one member of each group has the following questions that will serve as prompts for today's discussion. Take approximately 10 minutes for each of the three points, and do everything in your power to encourage your group to speak and express their opinions.

1 - Christ at the center. Read Colossians 1:15-20
- What implications do Paul's words in Colossians 1:15 have for your life today: "Christ is the image of the invisible God"?
- In what ways could a church become unfocused if it forgets what Colossians 1:18 says: "He is the head of the body, the church"?

2 - The things from above. Read Colossians 3:1-4
- How do you interpret the words of Colossians 3:1?
- Does God want us to evade our earthly responsibilities and focus only on the heavenly things that are coming to us?
- What role does "Christ sitting at the right hand of God" play in that verse?

3 - A new life. Read Colossians 3:5-11
- What does Paul mean by "putting to death" everything related to the old nature?
- What daily measures could we take so that the Spirit will end up prevailing in the constant internal struggle we have between our two natures?

Conclusions (10 minutes)

Colossians makes it clear that Christ is before everything, and that everything was created by Him and for Him. Everything we want to see of God we will find in Christ, because He is the image of the invisible God.

We must not forget that He is the true head of the church. In a church we should never put too much respect, admiration, or praise anyone but Christ. No human authority in our churches is the head. Only Christ.

We need to keep our eyes on the things from above (right where Christ is!) while keeping our feet on the ground. Paul does not invite us to evade reality or our obligations. On the contrary, he exhorts us to be excellent in what we do by focusing on the things that really matter, things that are transcendent.

When we focus our eyes on the right thing—or in this case, on the right person—it allows us to leave behind that which belonged to another life, to another moment, to another criteria that we used to have before we received the new divine nature through the Holy Spirit.

You can close this lesson with a song that speaks of Christ and exalts who He is. You can play a video or simply the audio and your group to pray while they listen.

Give each participant a copy of Readings from Colossians, downloadable at www.e625.com/lessons.

Lesson 41 > 1 TIMOTHY AND TITUS

The letter to Timothy is the first of two letters that Paul wrote to the man he treated and raised as a son. Timothy was the son of Eunice and grandson of Lois, who had taught him the Scriptures from a very young age. In the first letter, Paul gives Timothy pastoral instructions about his young apprentice's life mission. The letter is not long, but it is deep in theological truths. Most likely because Timothy was very familiar with Paul's theology, Paul did not go into great detail while addressing topics such as the purpose of the law (1:5-11), salvation (1:14-16, 2:4-6), the attributes of God (1:17), the fall (2:13-14), the Person of Christ (3:16, 6:15-16) and the second coming of Christ (6:14-15). Titus was another of Paul's beloved ministerial sons, which is why we are looking at these two letters together. Titus faced opposition from men in the churches he ministered to in Crete, presumably because he also was young, so both epistles have much in common.

Introductory questions (10 minutes)

After a brief introduction in which you explain in your own words what you have just read, have the students participate by asking some general questions.

1. Have you ever felt underestimated due to being young?

2. What is the best way to be heard when we want older or more experienced people to listen to us and change their opinion or behavior?

Age can be a great obstacle to being heard in a congregation, especially when we want to emphasize that something needs to change. The manner, the appropriateness, and the spirit with which things are said will increase our chances of being heard in our congregations.

Development (30 minutes)

The book of Timothy is a pastoral book with precise instructions, guidelines, and calls to attention for the leadership of the church..

The structure of Timothy's letter is as follows:

1. Instructions against false doctrine (1:1-20)
2. General recommendations to the church (2:1-3:16)
3. Instructions regarding false prophets (4:1-16)
4. Pastoral responsibilities (5:1-6:2)

5. The dangers facing the follower of God (6:3-21)

And Titus's:

1. Greetings and Titus' mission (1:1-16)
2. Sound doctrine (2:1-15)
3. The conduct of the believer (3:1-15)

Activity: Tell it to the Church

The following are a series of instructions Paul gave to Timothy and Titus regarding teaching in the church. Partner up with a few other people around you and act out how you would share this instruction with the church today.

One person will play the role of Timothy or Titus and the rest will play the role of the elders or church authorities.

Paul's instructions:
- Beware of False Doctrine (1:3-11)
- The Importance of Prayer (2:1-8)
- The Role of Women (2:9-15)
- The Requirements for Leaders (3:1-13)
- False Teachers (4:1-16)
- Responsibility to Widows (5:3-16)
- Responsibility to Elders (5:17-25)
- The Danger of Loving Money (6:6-10)

In the letter to Titus:
- Recognizing the Elders (1:5-9)
- Holy Living (2:1-10)
- Sound Doctrine (2:11-15)

Exercises in Piety:

1 Timothy 4:8
Is physical exercise good? Of course it is; it is our duty and responsibility to take care of the temple God gave each of us: our body. Paul tells Timothy that exercise is good, but that just as he practices physical exercise, he should also practice exercising piety toward others.

When starting to exercise, it's wise to begin with short, simple exercises before building up to more demanding ones that require more strength and endurance.

Similarly, let us begin by doing small works of faith. We will increase our works of faith until we become like Jesus.

Question for us: What small exercise of faith could you do this week?
Some ideas: helping others, defending a classmate, teaching someone something they don't know, etc.

Conclusions (10 minutes)

Teaching those older than us is quite a challenge, but if we do this with love and respect, recognizing that everyone is susceptible to being reprimanded, it will allow us to raise our hand in our congregation and promote positive change, rather than being complacent or complaining behind the scenes.

God calls young people to the mission of building up His church and being active parts of protecting it.

Give each participant a copy of Readings from 1 Timothy and Titus, downloadable at www.e625.com/lessons.

Lesson 42 > 2 TIMOTHY

This letter was written by Paul to Timothy from a cold and solitary cell. The Romans had imprisoned Paul for the second time and he knew that it was going to be the final one, since he would soon be executed and led to martyrdom.

Although Paul wrote to Timothy urging him to hurry to Rome, we do not know if Timothy managed to get there before Paul's execution.

Knowing that his end on this earth was near, Paul wrote to Timothy asking him to remain faithful in his duties (1:6), remain in sound doctrine (1:13-14), accept persecution for the gospel (2:3-4, 3:10-12), and trust in the Scriptures and preach them tirelessly (3:15, 4:5).

Introductory questions (10 minutes)

After a brief introduction in which you explain in your own words what you have just read, have the students participate by asking some general questions.

1. What characteristics do you think a person must have to be approved by God?
2. In this letter Paul speaks about foolish and senseless arguments and asks Timothy to stay away from them (2:23). How can you recognize when you are entering into a foolish and senseless argument? What is the best way to avoid them?

Development (30 minutes)

Knowing the end of his time on earth was near, Paul wanted to leave some final instructions to his beloved son in the faith, Timothy. This letter was written with a sense of urgency.

Its structure is as follows:

- Exhort Timothy to revive God's gift (1:3-7)
- Do not be ashamed of bearing witness to the gospel (1:8-11)
- Comparisons, such as soldier, athlete, and farmer (2:1-7)
- Invitation to be an approved worker (2:14-26)
- Ungodliness in the last days (3:1-9)
- Personal instructions (4:9-18)

Activity: I am not ashamed of the gospel.
At this point, Paul was in prison for the second time and most people had left him alone. He wrote this second letter to his beloved Timothy to ask him to come visit. Even though Paul was imprisoned and in a very difficult situation, he told Timothy he should not be ashamed or intimidated because the gospel is the power of God. God did not give us a Spirit of fear, but of power, love, and self-control.

Divide students into groups of three. Ask them to share in those groups if they have ever been ashamed to share the gospel with other people.

Ask the large group: What is the best way to share the gospel with our non-Christian acquaintances?

Activity: Flee.
One of Paul's instructions to Timothy is to flee from the evil passions of youth so that he can present himself as a worker approved by God. He asks Timothy not to get involved in foolish and senseless discussions that end up in fights (2:22-23).

Sometimes fleeing requires creating a plan for what you will do in difficult scenarios that are likely to unfold—this can help you be prepared to react appropriately when the time comes. With the same small group, discuss what actions you could take to flee from improper situations or senseless discussions.

For the discussion, focus on an example of an improper action or a senseless discussion from which we should flee.

Conclusions (10 minutes)
Paul asked Timothy to seek to live a righteous life so that he would not be ashamed to preach the gospel, because this is the POWER of God for salvation.
What a great task the Lord has left us through this letter, to be able to imitate this example!

Give each participant a copy of Readings from 2 Timothy, downloadable at www.e625.com/lessons.

Lesson 43 > 1 PETER

This letter was written by Peter in the midst of increasing persecution of the church. The purpose of this letter was to help the church to live in the midst of adversity without losing hope and without becoming bitter. This letter encourages followers of Christ to cast all anxiety on Him and trust in the Lord, believing He will return at the second coming.

Introductory questions (10 minutes)

After a brief introduction in which you explain in your own words what you have just read, have the students participate by asking some general questions.

1. Why does gold have to go through fire to be molded?
2. What do we know about the persecution of the church?sia?

Development (30 minutes)

The structure of 1 Peter is as follows:

- Remember our great salvation (1:3-2:10)
- Remember our example before men (2:11-4:6)
- Remember that our Lord will return (4:7-4:11)

Activity: Being Holy

Peter exhorts young people to behave intelligently by having self-control, while also recognizing what God has saved them from.

In groups of three, let us imagine a scenario in which you would need to act with wisdom in order to escape from a temptation or difficult situation. Discuss a strategy to combat or avoid that situation.

Activity: Not being ashamed

Peter writes, "But if anyone suffers because he is a Christian, let him not be ashamed, but let him praise God for bearing the name of Christ." Sometimes, people make fun of us for saying we are Christians or for doing what Jesus told us to do. When this happens, Peter encourages us not to be ashamed but to praise God, because God rejoices with us.

Discuss with your group of three what your response would be if someone mocked you for being a Christian. Share an experience where you have suffered for being Christian.

Activity: Young people submit to the elders
Peter encourages young people to obey their elders and take advantage of their experience, considering them worthy, and approaching them openly and without pride.

Make a list of three older people you respect and admire. Share it with your group and tell them why you admire them.

Conclusions (10 minutes)
Peter emphasizes our salvation because understanding that God saved us from a meaningless way of living gives us greater strength in the face of trials and temptations.

Peter emphasizes that the Christian life saves us from ourselves and asks us to seek holiness by leaving behind the pride of believing life can make sense without God. He concludes that we cannot be ashamed of the gospel and should live into a life of gratitude to God.

Give each participant a copy of Readings from 1 Peter, downloadable at www.e625.com/lessons.

Lesson 44 > 2 PETER

2 Peter was written to denounce false teachers who were trying to mislead the church. Peter's intention was to instruct the church on how to react to these false teachings.

The word "knowledge" appears at least 16 times in this short, three-chapter letter. This emphasizes Peter's belief that one must have knowledge of the Scriptures in order to be able to discern false doctrines.

There is also an explanation in this letter about the second coming of Jesus Christ. The people at the time had begun to doubt and deny the deity of Jesus.

Introductory questions (10 minutes)

After a brief introduction in which you explain in your own words what you have just read, have the students participate by asking some general questions..

1. Have you ever heard someone share a self-proclaimed Christian doctrine that didn't seem to be based on love? Do you think this was really a Christian way of belief?
2. How can you recognize a false teacher of the Word?a?

Development (30 minutes)

Have a volunteer read 2 Peter 1:5-12 aloud.

Peter wanted to encourage the church to study the truth. He wrote the following: "That is why I will always remind you of these things, even though you already know them and are established in the truth you now have."

Sometimes we might feel like there's no point studying a Bible story we're already familiar with, or think it's unnecessary to memorize Bible verses. Peter says that these things are essential even if we already feel familiar with the Bible. Having deep biblical knowledge is one of the ways we can discern whether what others say is true or not. Many false prophets have wanted to teach wrong things in the church. Peter knew the only way for followers of Christ not to believe the false teachers was for them to know the truth by understanding God's Word.

Divide into groups and have them make a list of Bible verses they have memorized. If you think this will be fun and meaningful for most of your students, you can make this a competition between groups. The group that knows the most verses by heart will win. Or, you can encourage students to choose a verse or two they would like to memorize and make a plan to do so.

The apostle Peter insists on the importance of knowing the Bible. When we know the Bible well, no one—not even people in the church, who might teach falsely even though they have good intentions—can deceive us.

Activity: The Day of the Lord
Peter describes what the second coming of the Lord Jesus Christ will be like, giving a narrative description of that day.

Since everything will be destroyed as described, should we not live according to God's commands, conducting ourselves blamelessly and eagerly awaiting the coming of the day of the Lord? On that day the heavens will be destroyed by fire, and everything will melt with the heat of the flames.

Discuss with your group the meaning of the description from Peter in Chapter 3, from the point of view of astronomy.

Conclusions (10 minutes)
We need to diligently and urgently study the Scriptures, meditating on them and seeking to practice them constantly. There will always be people who distort Scripture and preach against love. Study and be zealous with the truth, always keeping in mind that mercy and love are the central foundation of our message.

Give each participant a copy of Readings from 2 Peter, downloadable at www.e625.com/lessons.

Lesson 45 > JUDE

This book was not written by Judas the traitor, but by Jesus' half-brother. His name comes from "Judah," which means praise.

Jude is a short writing that is along the same lines as the message of 2 Peter. It rejects false teachers and false doctrines, but it includes something surprising: Jude did not recognize Jesus as the Messiah (John 7:1-9) until after seeing him resurrected (Acts 1:14). His own half-brother didn't recognize him! Sometimes, we have a hard time recognizing the potential of the people we know best.

After his conversion and recognizing Jesus as the Messiah, Jude became a strong advocate of sound doctrine and a fierce fighter against false doctrines, describing apostates vividly, noting that those with disordered personal lives cannot be connected with correct and healthy teachings.

Introductory questions (10 minutes)

After a brief introduction in which you explain in your own words what you have just read, have the students participate by asking some general questions.

1. What does the word apostasy mean? (Read the definition from the dictionary once they have answered.)
1. What relationship should there be between the message and the way of life of those who preach?

Development (30 minutes)

The structure of this book is as follows:
1. Condemnation against apostates (3, 4)
2. Consequences of apostates (5, 6)
3. Characteristics of apostates (8-16)
4. Defenses against apostasies (17-23)
5. Doxology

To Say and to Do
Have a volunteer read Jude 1:12-14

Invite everyone to stand up. Tell them that for the next few minutes they must imitate what you say and not what you do, and that they must respond immediately.

For example:
You say "jump" and you jump. Everyone else must jump. But then you say "sit" while you remain standing...and whoever remains standing loses.

What this game shows us is that it is very difficult to follow instructions when you say one thing and do something very different.

Jude's invitation is for us to hear the message and meditate on it, but also to compare and contrast it with the way of life of the leaders and those who are giving the message. The Bible itself encourages us to distrust those who say one thing but live otherwise.

Reflection on money
Now have a volunteer read Jude 1:11.
Historically there has been strong criticism of the church when money is mentioned, and here Jude strongly exhorts us not to do things "just to make money." This coincides with what Paul said to Timothy when he explained that the love of money is the root of all kinds of evil.

Help your group to think by asking:
Is money the problem that Jude and Timothy are denouncing?
The problem is greed.

Separate the group into two teams.

Have each group work together to describe what they think are biblical and God-honoring practices in the relationship between money and ministry. How would they describe incorrect practices in this relationship?
We will do this with a respectful spirit, remembering mercy and love as the main points of our message and our group.

Conclusions (10 minutes)

Teachers and leaders must have authority, which is more than just saying the right things. Authority is earned by being consistent in what we say and what we do. Jude's letter makes it clear that there will always be people with false motivations. That is why it is important to be sure of what is right, and what is not part of God's message, regardless of how good it feels or how well people speak.

Give each participant a copy of Readings from Jude at www.e625.com/lessons.

Lesson 46 › HEBREWS

Although many believe that the author of Hebrews was Paul, we do not know for sure who wrote this letter. We do know that the letter clearly states that through faith in Jesus we have direct access to God.

The book's name comes from the fact that it was written with a clear focus on the Jews and explains concepts that a Jewish audience of the time would have understood perfectly, such as calling Jesus the lamb that fulfills the law of Moses for the atonement of sins. The verses of this text recall many concepts of the Old Testament that the Jewish culture could understand very well, such as the veil that was torn, or the heroes of faith in the history of Israel in chapter 11.

Hebrews begins as a sermon and includes an eloquent explanation of why Christ is the fulfillment of the Old Testament.

Introductory questions (10 minutes)

After a brief introduction in which you explain in your own words what you have just read, have the students participate by asking some general questions.

1. What do you think faith is?
2. Which symbols and figures in the Old Testament attract your attention the most?
3. Why is Jesus called a lamb?

Development (30 minutes)

The structure of this book is as follows:
1. Jesus Christ's position
2. Jesus' priesthood (4:14-7:28, 8:1-10:18)
3. The believer's faith (10:19-12:29)
4. Our relationship with others and with God (13:1-21)

The torn veil

Divide your group into even teams. Each team will be given a piece of cloth. Each team must stretch their cloth until it tears and splits in two. You cannot use anything but your own strength to do this.

Just as this piece of cloth was torn, so was the veil that separated the people from the presence of God. Jesus came to tear that veil and give people access to the holiest One. Jesus fulfilled the law completely. He had to do this in order to serve as high priest and intercede for us before the Father. The author of Hebrews says that people now do not have a high priest unable to sympathize with our weaknesses, but rather have one who has been tempted in every way just as we are, yet is without sin. So, let us approach the throne of grace with confidence, so that we may receive mercy and find grace to help us in our time of need (Hebrews 4:15-16).

Activity:
Have three different volunteers read Hebrews 11:1-2-3.

The letter to the Hebrews defines faith as the assurance of things hoped for, the certainty of things not seen.

In the Old Testament there are many examples of people of faith: Abel, Enoch, Noah, Abraham, Isaac, Jacob, Joseph, Moses, Rahab, Gideon and more. Many of them were people with weaknesses and good attributes, but all of them had faith. They were certain that God was with them, even though none of them knew Jesus. We have the privilege of being able to have faith and know that Jesus is the Son of God

Let's make a small learning analogy. Think for a moment about which hero of the faith most resembles your life or the moment you are going through today. Select who you picked and why with the group.

For example, you might share that you are trusting God for a miracle, and when you see your current situation you know that what you hope for is only possible through God. This is very similar to what Abraham went through when he was told that he was going to be the father of multitudes, despite being very old and having a wife who biologically could no longer have children. He had faith in God, and God gave him a miracle.

Conclusions (10 minutes)

It is beautiful to think about how we can learn from those who came before us. Today we can stand the shoulders of the giants of faith and hope who came before us, learning from them and following in their example. We might also see this in our leaders, families, and friends.

The greatest sacrifice and work of faith was made by Jesus at calvary when He gave Himself as the lamb in atonement for our sins. Thanks to His great work of faith, we can enter confidently into the presence of our glorious God today.

Give each participant a copy of Readings from Hebrews, downloadable at www.e625.com/lessons.

Lesson 47 > 1 JOHN

The First Epistle of John was written by John, the Beloved Disciple, and is the first of three letters he wrote. Since it does not have a specific recipient, it is said to be a general epistle. When John wrote this epistle, a movement known as Gnosticism had been born, which denied the incarnation of Jesus Christ and was spreading false doctrines, including that salvation was given through knowledge and that the body and the spirit were separate. Because of this, John wrote with the authority of a father to warn the church against these teachings and to encourage his readers in love. John thus sought to strengthen basic but profound concepts within the church.

When we read John in each of his writings—the Gospel of John, First, Second, and Third John, and Revelation—we can see the zeal with which he defended God's supreme plan through the redemptive work of Jesus.

The three fundamental factors of true spirituality that John explains are: 1) A correct belief in Jesus, which produces 2) an obedience to His commandments by putting them into action, which manifests 3) in our love for God and our brethren. These three elements (faith in Jesus, obedience, and love) produce the fruit of spirituality in our lives.

Introductory questions (10 minutes)

After a brief introduction in which you explain in your own words what you have just read, have the students participate by asking some general questions.

1. What is love?
2. How can we know if someone loves God?
3. What does the word "friend" mean?

Development (30 minutes)

The structure of this book is as follows:
1. Characteristics of having communion with God (1)
2. Obedience to God's commandments (2)
3. Call to a new commandment (2:8)
4. The relationship between parents and children (2:12-14)
5. The relationship with the world (2:15-17)
6. Beware of antichrists (2:18-27)
7. Knowing the great love of God (3)
8. Remaining in love (4)

9. Living in the faith

Loving with deeds
Have a volunteer read aloud 1 John 3:16-18.

John spoke of a new commandment, which is to love our brothers with a love like the love of Jesus. When John said that we should give our lives for our brothers, he did not necessarily mean dying for our brothers. This refers to helping our brothers and sisters with whatever we have at our disposal. If someone asks you for help, help them. This demonstrates God's love to them. John said, "If someone who has material goods sees his brother in need and has no compassion for him, how can it be said that the love of God dwells in him? Dear children, let us not love in word or in lip service, but in deed and in truth."

In discussion groups, talk about how you have been helped or have helped other people. How have you shown or been shown the Love of God?

As Christians we must understand that this is the central message of the gospel: God is love. Love is evident in our actions. No one can say they love God if they hate their brother.

The New Commandment
Read aloud 1 John 2:8.

This letter was most likely written to the church in the last years of the first century. Christians had been listening to the teachings of the apostles for quite some time. Why does John insist that this is a new commandment?

In discussion groups we will use the teaching of John to answer the following questions.

What is the NEW commandment John taught? What is new about this commandment?

(Read John 13 to find the answer)

John emphasizes the importance of loving our brothers and sisters in a real and genuine way.

According to 1 John 3, what happens to someone who does not show love to his brother or sister?

These two questions could take us entire days to process. It is amazing that there was a new commandment, taught by Jesus Himself and then reinforced by John in the last years of his life. Jesus had already said that the law was summarized in these two commandments: Love God with all our strength, and our neighbor as ourselves. Jesus' statement that he would teach a NEW commandment is deeply meaningful for those of us who are His disciples.

Conclusions (10 minutes)

The love of God is demonstrated with deeds and expressed with actions that respond to the needs of others. These actions allow us to speak with authority.

In the modern world and especially in the traditional educational system, we often are taught the theory first and then given the opportunity to practice. John (newer educational techniques) show us that the correct way to learn is the other way around. Most of the things you have learned spring from experimentation and then the acquisition of theory. Think of how you learned to drive or play video games. To teach about God's love, let's start with actions first. Through those actions we will gain the correct emotions to continue loving. Close with a prayer.

Give each participant a copy of Readings from 1 John at www.e625.com/lessons.

Lesson 48 › 2 AND 3 JOHN

These are the two shortest letters in the New Testament. In the second letter John re-emphasizes the message of his first letter about God's love among the followers of Christ, referencing the commandment to put love into practice. He also gives a strong warning against those who preach but do not recognize Jesus Christ as the son of God.

The third letter is addressed to John's friend Gaius. John is happy with Gaius' behavior and life testimony, and exalts his reputation, while he rebukes the behavior of other people in the congregation.

Another topic discussed in this letter is hospitality, which is demonstrated by his friend Gaius, who shows appreciation to itinerant ministers and welcomes them into his home.

Introductory questions (10 minutes)

After a brief introduction in which you explain in your own words what you have just read, have the students participate by asking some general questions.

1. What does a "good testimony" mean?
2. Why do you think the Bible says that a good name is better than much gold?

Development (30 minutes)

La estructura de estas cartas es la siguiente:The structure of these letters is as follows:

2 John
1. Reminder of the commandment of love. (2 John 4-6)
2. Warning against deceivers. (2 John 7-11)
3. The longing to see his disciples. (2 John 12)

3 John
1. Recognition of Gaius' faithfulness. (3 John 1-8)
2. Denunciation of evil and call not to imitate it. (3 John 9-11)
3. The longing to see his disciples. (3 John 13)

Activity: Day of Testimonies

John again calls us to express love in actions. These actions are evidence that we love one another.

Our activity together now is to spend a good time sharing testimonies about the love of God expressed by our brothers and sisters toward us. We will ask those who have a testimony about how they have felt the love of God through their brothers and sisters in the faith to come forward. This is a call to attention for our groups, a reminder to us that the love of God generates plenty of evidence that can be shared and that enriches other people's faith. A congregation that has few testimonies of love among the brothers and sisters must review its doctrine and begin to be more emphatic in preaching about love.

Activity: Nominations

John writes his third letter to his friend Gaius, of whom he speaks very well and encourages him because of the good testimony of a Christian life that he has led.

In this activity, you will nominate a person to speak well about a friend within the congregation. The idea is to share about the good Christian behaviors through which this chosen friend showed their faith and love for God. When he or she finishes speaking and giving testimony of the friend, the friend in question will nominate another person who must share about another friend, and so on. The number of people who can be shared about (nominated) in this activity will depend on how much time you have in your meeting.

Conclusions (10 minutes)

John is the disciple who lived and practiced the gospel on earth the longest. His greatest teaching is that love is not a feeling, but a commitment to action. Love is not to be kept for ourselves. It is meant to be expressed, given, and multiplied. That is the great mission God gives His children.

Love has practical consequences, such as hospitality and friendship, and is not limited to returning a good deed with another good deed. God's kind of love means loving even those who do not deserve it, just as God loves all human beings.

Close with a circle of appreciation in which each person must say something encouraging to the next person. It may be a bit strange for some, but this is one practical way to express love that gets easier with practice. End your gathering in prayer.

Give each participant a copy of Readings from 2 and 3 John at www.e625.com/lessons.

Lesson 49> REVELATION (Part 1)

Revelation is about the end of the world or of history. It was written by John, most likely at the end of his life, around the decade of the '90s in the first century. As far as we know, John was the last of the apostles to die. While writing this letter he was exiled on the island of Patmos.

Revelation reveals a glorious and triumphant Christ despite all the obstacles of history. In this book Jesus is the faithful witness, the firstborn of the dead, the King of kings and Lord of lords, the alpha and the omega, the beginning and the end, the One who was and the One who is to come, the Almighty, the Son of Man, the One who lives forever and ever, the Son of God, holy and true, the Lion of Judah, the Lamb in heaven sitting on the throne, and the bright morning Star.

In the first part of this book, John writes to the churches he had pastored and overseen, wanting to see them continue to mature and grow.

Introductory questions (10 minutes)

After a brief introduction in which you explain in your own words what you have just read, have the students participate by asking some general questions.

1. What have you heard about Revelation?
2. What feeling does this book generate in you and why?

Development (35 minutes)

The outline of the first part of Revelation is as follows:

1. The vision of the glorified Christ and the commission to write the book (1:9-20)
2. The letters to the churches (2:1-3:22)
3. Worship in heaven (4:1-5:14)

Activities: The message to the churches

John writes to seven churches that were obviously under his care. These churches were in Asia. He has special words for each one:

1 - Ephesus (2:1-7)
     "You have left your first love."
2 - Smyrna (2:8-11)

"Be faithful until death, and I will give you the crown of life."
3 - Pergamum (2:12-17)
"I have a few things against you."
4 - Thyatira (2:18-29)
"Hold on to what you have until I come."
5 - Sardis (3:1-6)
"You have a reputation that you are alive, but you are dead."
6 - Philadelphia (3:7-13)
"I have set before you an open door."
7 - Laodicea (3:14-22)
"You are neither cold nor hot."

There is great value in thinking about these messages and bringing them into our current context. They are still relevant for us in our time. In small groups we will study the message to each of the churches and complete the following chart.

Let everyone see as an example the complete chart with Ephesus, and if possible divide your group into six smaller groups to complete the remaining charts.

Example:

Church:	Praise:	Criticism:	Instruction:	Promise:
Ephesus	Your deeds, your hard work, and your perseverance. You have not put up with the wicked. You have persevered and suffered for my name.	You have left your first love.	Do the works you did at the beginning.	The right to eat from the tree of life.
Smyrna				
Pergamum				
Thyatira				
Sardis				
Philadelphia				
Laodicea				

Download copies of this chart at www.e625.com/lessons.

Activity: Worship in Heaven
Have someone read Revelation chapter 4 out loud.

Have you ever imagined what worship in heaven will be like? In a vision, John saw a fragment of a worship service in heaven.

What he saw was impressive. There was a throne surrounded by 24 elders with golden crowns. Around the throne he saw four living creatures with different forms. All of them were saying, "Holy, Holy, Holy is the Lord God Almighty," who was, who is, and who is to come. Each time they worshiped, the 24 elders laid their crowns before the throne.

The worship in this scene was incredibly creative. One of the living creatures was shaped like a lion, another like a calf, another with a face like a man, and the fourth like a flying eagle.

Have the group choose four songs with the following characteristics.
The first song should have a reference to a lion. The second song has a more joyful character like a young calf. The third song should refer to our humanity, and the last one should have a tone of sublime worship. If you know of any that refers to an eagle, that's even better.

Conclusions (5 minutes)
God cares about the health of our churches. We cannot be satisfied with what we have already experienced: We must continue to mature and grow. We can barely imagine the glory of Christ or the worship in heaven. John lacked words and allegorical images to describe clearly what he saw.

Revelation speaks about the present and the future, interweaving the opportunities we have now and those we will have in God's glory. Have a volunteer close in prayer thanking God for His faithfulness.

Give each participant a copy of Readings from Revelation part 1 at www.e625.com/lessons.

Lesson 50 > REVELATION (Part 2)

The second part of the book of Revelation focuses on the pivotal events of the second coming of our Lord Jesus Christ. The descriptions and ideas in this final portion of the Bible have sparked the imagination of many, fear of others, and hope of those of us who believe that Jesus will return for His church.

This closing of the written revelation narrates the events from the great tribulation where the earth will see enormous destruction and suffering (6:1-18:24) to the great white throne of judgment (20:11-15), ending at the eternal reality where God is everything (21:1-22:21).

Introductory questions (10 minutes)

After a brief introduction in which you explain in your own words what you have just read, have the students participate by asking some general questions.

1. What have you heard about the great tribulation, the second coming of Jesus, and the final judgment?
2. What do people usually believe about these events?
3. What do you feel when you speak about these things?

Development (40 minutes)

The structure of the second part of Revelation is:

1. The great tribulation (6:1-18:24)
2. The return of the King (19:1-21)
3. The millennium (20:1-10)
4. The judgment from the great white throne (20:11-15)
5. The eternal state (21:1-22:21)

Activity: The events as they will be

For this exercise, make sure you have some extra Bibles and the rest of the materials mentioned.

A significant part of Revelation focuses on the time of tribulation and judgment that will happen on earth. John narrates the destruction that accompanies the opening of each seal. He also narrates the appearance of angels with trumpets followed by horsemen of God. The number of scenes appearing from chapter 6 to chapter 21 is impressive, worthy of several movies.

Divide the participants into smaller groups. Assign them to look for the most important events mentioned in these chapters, draw or write about them, and arrange them in chronological order. Give them large sheets of paper and markers so that they can create an illustrated timeline of the key events and the most relevant scenes narrated from chapter six to chapter 21.

You can reward the most creative and complete chronological timelines. Not every timeline is going to match up, and that is to be expected. In Revelation, John is describing a reality he did not have enough tools to fully understand. What each of these scenes means and their order has been discussed by great teachers from all over the world throughout the centuries.

In advance of your time together, prepare by reading Bible commentaries and reference books, accepting that the order of some events or what kind of people are represented in each scene have different interpretations according to different denominations. It is also a good idea to research what interpretation is accepted by your denomination or local church and why, so you can explain it to your young people.

Conclusions (10 minutes)

Beyond the possible scenarios regarding the final events, what is not debatable is that there will be a final judgment for all human beings and that the only possibility of being found righteous is through Christ. He will return for those who have trusted in Him by faith, those who are His people, and the goodness and glory of God will have its final triumph against evil and the kingdom of darkness.

Close the lesson with a message of hope. Christ returns for His church and the final promise of His Word is the complete glory that we will be able to enjoy with Him.

Give each participant a copy of Readings from Revelation Part 2 at www.e625.com/lessons.

NOTES

NOTES

NOTES

NOTES

NOTES

WHO IS BEHIND THIS BOOK??

Specialties 625 is a team of pastors and servants from different countries, different denominations, belonging to churches of different sizes and styles, who love Christ and the new generations.

e625.com

WHAT IS E625.COM ABOUT?

Our passion is to help families and churches to find good materials and resources to aid in the discipleship of new generations, and that is why our website serves parents, pastors, teachers and leaders 365 days a year through **www.e625.com** with free resources.

zona de contenido
PREMIUM

WHAT IS THE PREMIUM SERVICE?

In addition to free reflections and short materials, we have a service that includes lessons, series, investigations, online guides, and audiovisual resources to facilitate your tasks. Your church can access this with a monthly subscription to this service per congregation that allows all leaders of a local church to download materials to share as a team and make the necessary copies that they find relevant for the different activities of the congregation or their families.

CAN I TEAM UP WITH YOU?

It would be a privilege to help you, and our formal education possibilities exist with that objective in mind. Visit **www.e625.com/Eventos** to find out about our seminars and events, and enter **www.institutoE625.com** to learn about the online courses offered by the E 6.25 Institute.

DO YOU WANT UPDATES?

Register now for the updates of **e625.com** depending on your work environment: Children- Middle School - High School - Young Adults.

LET'S LEARN TOGETHER!

Magazine
Books
Chat
Downloads
Subscription
Store
Events
Seminars
Online Education
www.InstitutoE625.com
e625.com